CONTENTS

D1138626

SYMBOLS & ABBREVIATIONS

The following symbols are used throughout this book:

ⓐ address   ⓣ telephone   ⓕ fax   ⓔ email   ⓦ website address
ⓛ opening times   ⓝ public transport connections   ⓘ important

The following symbols are used on the maps:

🛈	information office	◯	city
✈	airport	○	large town
➕	hospital	◦	small town
🚓	police station	═	motorway
🚌	bus station	—	main road
🚆	railway station	—	minor road
✝	cathedral	—	railway
❶	numbers denote featured cafés & restaurants		

Hotels and restaurants are graded by approximate price as follows:
£ budget   ££ mid-range   £££ expensive

▶ *Bologna 'la rossa' – the red-hued city*

INTRODUCING
Bologna

Introduction

Emilia-Romagna, the heartland of northern Italy, has always played second fiddle to its neighbour Tuscany, which has long attracted tourists because of the treasures of Florence, Siena and Pisa. But Bologna, the capital of the region, is one of the most refined and enticing cities in the country, a fact that more people are beginning to discover as low-cost airlines head there. What's more, it has considerably fewer crowds.

Before being controlled by the papacy, and then brought under Italian Unification, the region was ruled by a range of powerful and wealthy aristocratic dynasties – the d'Este family in Ferrara and Modena, the Farnese in Parma, the Bentivoglios in Bologna and lesser dynasties in Ravenna and Rimini. Their legacies can still be seen in the many surviving magnificent Renaissance courts, castles and fortresses, as well as a few remaining towers that indicated their importance.

Bologna is also a city of *portici* (porticoes or arcades). Reportedly there are over 60 km (40 miles) of these covered walkways, which allow business, shopping and socialising to be carried out in all weathers in the historic centre, providing shade during the torrid summers and shelter during the rainy winters.

Bologna's *centro storico* (historic centre) has been recognised as the largest intact historical urban core in the world, and it is possible to admire important structures from the Roman period, remnants of the original medieval walls that used to surround the city, as well as vaults, arches and corbels from the 12th and 14th centuries.

But it is the city's reputation as a home to freethinkers that really established its fame. It is known, among other things, as

Bologna la Dotta (the 'Learned'), as its university, established in the 11th century, is the oldest in Europe. *Bologna la Rossa* (the 'Red') was a phrase originally coined to describe the red-hued buildings of the city, but was also reckoned to refer to the Communist tendencies of those living in the region. *Bologna la Grassa* (the 'Fat') is equally fitting. Food is sacred to the Bolognese, and the region's cuisine is respected throughout the country. That is hardly surprising when the region has produced some of Italy's most famous gastronomic delights, including Parmesan cheese, Parma ham and lasagne.

Away from the city, the poplar-studded landscape starts at the foothills of the Apennine mountains in the south and extends to the northern plain, the Pianura Padana. This has been a wheat-growing area since Roman times, and today its industry and agricultural businesses are Italy's most prosperous, making Emilia-Romagna one of the richest regions in Italy. This, in turn, lends Bologna and the whole area a sophisticated air – expect locals to be both well dressed and well mannered.

Cutting through the middle of the region, the Via Aemilia (or A1 and A14) is a Roman military road constructed in 187 BC as part of the pilgrims' route to Rome and the way east to Ravenna and Venice. The towns that developed along the Via Aemilia – including Piacenza and Modena – are some of Italy's most dramatic. Other towns easily accessible from Bologna are Parma, a wealthy provincial town famous for its architecture, Ferrara, which has an important Renaissance centre, and Ravenna, where you will find the world's best-preserved Byzantine mosaics.

When to go

SEASONS & CLIMATE

Unlike many destinations, there are no hard-and-fast rules about when to plan a visit to Bologna – each season offers something different. That said, the months of July and, in particular, August can be uncomfortably hot; during the latter many locals head to the mountains or the coast, leaving many shops and restaurants closed for the entire month. The city is at its most crowded during Christmas, Easter and the Festa di San Luca in May (see page 10), but it's also at its most vibrant, so if you don't mind the throng these can be wonderful times to visit. To get the best out of the city, however, without excessive heat or crowds, aim to visit in spring or autumn. During March and April, and September and October, the air is warm, with an average temperature of 17°C (63°F), the skies are (usually) blue and the flowers in bloom.

PUBLIC HOLIDAYS

New Year's Day 1 January

Epiphany 6 January

Easter Late March to early April

Liberation Day and St Mark's Feast Day 25 April

Labour Day 1 May

Ferragosto (Assumption of the Blessed Virgin Mary) 15 August

All Saints' Day 1 November

Immaculate Conception of the Blessed Virgin 8 December

Christmas Day 25 December

Santo Stefano (Boxing Day) 26 December

If you do visit in summer, make sure you wear lightweight fabrics such as cotton or linen, a hat and sunblock, and rehydrate regularly with bottled water. Italians take their midday siesta seriously for a reason – between 12.00 noon and 15.00 the heat is intense, so if you don't want to waste time sleeping, use this time to visit shady museums or churches (if they are open) and keep out of the sun. Sturdy walking shoes are advisable at any time of year as the flag-stoned streets can be unforgiving on high heels or lightweight soles.

ANNUAL EVENTS

There are literally hundreds of festivals year-round throughout the Emilia-Romagna region, and some of the most enjoyable are the smaller local affairs rather than flashy national events. Below are some of the highlights, but it's always best to check with local tourist offices about what's going on during your visit, as many dates are liable to change from year to year.

Like all Italians, the Bolognese take their festivals very seriously, and a large part of the annual activities have their roots in the Catholic faith, still so central to the country. Christmas, and in particular Holy Week – the run-up to Easter – are huge events, as is the February Carnival marking the period of Lent.

Particular to the region in this gastronomic heartland is the emphasis on food; almost every festival in and around Bologna will be accompanied by vast displays of local delicacies to be enjoyed by all.

February

Carnivale The whole of Italy celebrates the 40-day period of Lent with this carnival, featuring masked balls, parades and other festivities, but there are also certain aspects specific to the Emilia-Romagna region·

Festival of Santo Apollonia at Bellaria-Igea Marina (9–14th).
Mardi Gras Carnival and fun at Borgo Tossignano, Bologna.
Shrove Tuesday carnival San Giovanni in Persiceto, Bologna.

March
Ravioli Festival Casalfiumanese Bologna (2nd or 3rd Sunday).
Fiera del Bue Grasso Festival of the 'Fat Ox' at Cavriago, an ancient cattle fair with food tastings and craft demonstrations (25–27th).

Around Easter
Pagnotta di Pasqua is dedicated to the traditional Easter cake (Palm Sunday).
Holy Week The week leading up to Easter is celebrated with Masses in all the churches of the region.
Festival of Piadine A pie festival in which dough rounds filled with ham or cheese, a speciality of the region, are served (Easter Monday).

April
Vulandra kite and kitemakers' festival Ferrara (3rd & 4th weekends).
Formula 1 Grand Prix of San Marino The show comes to Imola (late April to early May).

May
Festa della Matricola, Bologna. University students gather to enrol in Piazza Maggiore then celebrate in costumes and drunken revelry (15th).
Festa di San Luca The image of the Virgin is brought down to Bologna from the Santuario di San Luca on Ascension Day.
'Marriage to the Sea', Ceriva. Ceremony celebrating Ascension Day. Festivities and a regatta.

Palio di Ferrara Horse racing and Renaissance pageantry in Ferrara's ancient city centre (last Sunday in the month, moved to first Sunday in June if it rains).
Balsamic vinegar festival The pride of Modena is celebrated in restaurants and through cookery classes (late May to early June).

June
Renaissance Festival, Castel del Rio (last weekend of June).
Palio del Niballo, Faenza. One of the most spectacular horseback tournaments in the region, complete with 16th-century costumes (last Sunday).
Ravenna Music Festival Opera, classical music and ballet in the churches, and purportedly the world's oldest jazz festival (mid-June to mid-July).

July
Ferrara sotto le stelle Ferrara rock festival.
Ravenna Jazz Festival (last two weeks).

August
Assumption of the Blessed Virgin Mary Festivals are held throughout the region to celebrate this important date in the religious calendar (15th).

September
Sausage Festival Takes place at Gaggio Montano, Bologna (first Sunday).
Parma Ham Festival The local delicacy is honoured at Langhirano (first week).

Settembre Dantesco, Ravenna. Readings and events dedicated to Dante, culminating on 10 September, the anniversary of his death.
Wine festival, San Pietro in Vincoli. One of the region's largest wine festivals (late September).

October
Truffle festival Calestano, Parma. An opportunity to sample the luscious delicacies (last Saturday in the month).

November
Sangiovese wine week, Imola (2nd week).

December
Most towns and villages construct their own Nativity scene in the run-up to Christmas. The larger towns also stage Christmas markets where nativity figurines and decorations can be bought.
Santa Lucia Festival Pottery fairs and fun at Forlì and Savignano (13th).
New Year's Eve Masses are celebrated in churches, firework displays are held and broken crockery is tossed from balconies marking the end of the year. In Bologna there is also the parade of the *bue grasso* (fat ox).

▶ *Maybe plan your trip to coincide with a local* palio

PALIO PIÙ ANTICO DEL MONDO
CHI GIOCHI DELLE BANDIERE ESTENSI, CORTEO STORICO
CORSE DEL PALIO ED ALTRI SUGGESTIVI EVENTI

ARA 8·14-15-16·22·30 M

Palios

Palios (bareback horse races) have been a feature of the northern Italian landscape since medieval times, when the troubled relations between different districts meant that the military needed to keep their equestrian skills up to scratch. The races, therefore, were created as much for serious practical reasons as they were for showmanship and local pride.

Italy's most famous *palio* takes place in Siena in Tuscany, but the Emilia-Romagna region has more than its fair share of races to entertain the crowds. One of the best is also the oldest in Italy – the **Palio di San Giorgio** in Ferrara, which takes place on the last Sunday in May. Riders, dressed in medieval costume, representing each of the eight districts (known as *contrade*) gallop through the city streets. All are vying for the *palio*, a brightly coloured flag that is the coveted first prize. (Traditionally, the second prize is a suckling pig and the third a chicken.) It's a high-octane event, with the pavements lined with cheering supporters waving the coloured flag that represents 'their' district. Aside from the race itself, there are plenty of other festivities, most of them continuing with the medieval pageantry theme.

On the first Sunday in June, the **Palio of the Contrade** takes place in Parma to commemorate the wedding, in 1523, of Pietro Maria Rossi III to Camilla Gonzaga of Mantova. The bride and bridegroom came from two of the region's aristocratic families, which are still in existence today. The race culminates with a sumptuous banquet and a parade with thousands of people waving flags and winding their way through the streets of the town.

Although these races are firmly rooted in their medieval traditions, today they are also an excuse for partying, socialising and a bit of fun. Besides the main event there will often be more light-hearted competitions, such as a *palio* on donkeys, and girls' and boys' races.

🔺 *The excitement of the* palios

History

The first settlers of northern and central Italy were the Etruscans; under the name Felsina, they founded the city that is now Bologna. They made much use of its strategic position, set as it is between the Mediterranean and Adriatic sea trading routes, as well as of its strong agricultural potential. But within just a few centuries the mighty power of the Roman Empire swept over the entire country and the Etruscan kings were no more. In the 2nd century BC the Romans renamed the city Bononia, and in time it grew in both size and wealth, eventually becoming the second most important city in Italy after Rome. After the fall of Rome, the landscape was ripe for new invaders, and in the 8th century the Lombards, moving south from what is now Germany and Austria, began to control much of the peninsula, including Bologna. Along with other cities such as Milan, Verona and Parma, Bologna joined the Lombard League, set up to protect against the advances of the Holy Roman Empire. As such they became city-states, with a relative degree of governmental autonomy.

The Lombards believed in culture as a route to wealth and success, and undoubtedly one of the most important events in Bologna's history was the establishment of a university in 1088 – it is the oldest in Europe. Bologna soon became renowned as a city of enlightenment and education, which in turn brought it much wealth and reputation. The great poets, Dante and Petrarch, are among those who could name the university as their alma mater. The Middle Ages were, in fact, the city's Golden Age, during which time the porticoed arcades, towers and churches were constructed, largely financed by the great families of the age such as the Bentivoglios and the Farnese. At this time much of Italy was also engaged in the battle for supremacy being waged between the Papal States and the Holy Roman Empire, which were both vying for overall control. While these powers were caught up in political machinations, the Lombards were able to concentrate on their own cities, thus developing them into far more important and successful centres.

By the 16th century, however, Bologna also became a Papal State, ruled from Rome, although in reality much of the governance was still controlled by the various aristocratic families that exercised considerable power over the region. Nevertheless, this was also another flourishing time for the city, particularly with the establishment of the Bolognese School, an art movement that saw the rise of the great baroque artists such as Carracci, Domenichino and Guercino, whose works can now be seen in the Pinacoteca Nazionale (see page 87).

Papal rule was abandoned when Napoleon conquered Italy in 1800, but this was also the dawning of a new age. The Italians, having been ruled at various times by Greeks, Germans, Spaniards and now French, were tired of being governed by foreigners, and were equally not keen to return to Vatican rule. This gave rise to the Risorgimento, the bid for a unified Italy. Bologna joined this campaign, becoming part of the Kingdom of Italy in 1859.

From that point until the present day Bologna has retained its highly cultured reputation and is considered one of Italy's most elegant and refined cities.

Lifestyle

'I long for Bologna...where the foreigners are overwhelmed by the warm welcome they are accorded ... in Bologna everything is beautiful, in both the material and moral sense... believe me, you really do encounter good-hearted people, they are everywhere.'

Giacomo Leopardi, poet and philosopher (1798–1837)

La Dotta, La Grassa and La Rossa (the Learned, the Fat and the Red) are Bologna's nicknames, but it is an insistence on plain truth that sets the Bolognese apart. In the 11th century it was the desire for truth and law that led to the founding of the University of Bologna. And it's the honest ingredients in the kitchen that have made Bolognese food and cuisine among the best in Italy, and the source of one of its nicknames, La Grassa. As for 'La Rossa', Bologna may be full of socialist virtue (its municipal government was long in the hands of the Italian Communist Party, now the PDS), but the city is also very wealthy. 'La Rossa' also refers to the red-coloured stucco of the city's buildings.

Even its automotive industry is classy, with the likes of Lamborghini and Ducati (motorcycles) headquartered here, and Maserati only recently moved to nearby Modena. Its political energy is fuelled by the 100,000 students living here, who give the city the air of a giant university campus, especially in good weather, when they fill the cafés and bars in every street and piazza.

For all Bologna's richly decorated churches, you'd hardly call it a pious city. Between the freethinking students and the leftward lean of its residents, the church is less of a dominating force here than elsewhere in Italy. Even the city's cultural offerings reflect its heady mix of tastes and styles, with everything from rap to jazz to Renaissance madrigals, as well as avant-garde ballet, theatre and art exhibitions on offer at almost any time of year.

Even in August, when Italy's month-long holidays empty the city as though someone had pulled the plug, enough students remain to keep the *centro storico* lively. Though rap and grunge may have replaced the more sedate strains of early 19th-century music, Giacomo Leopardi would still recognise the city.

⬥ *Food is very important to the Bolognese*

Culture

When Bologna was named a European City of Culture in 2000, it marked a much-needed turnaround in the attention that the city received. Long in the shadow of Rome, Florence, Venice and Milan, Bologna was seen as something of a backwater, but this in fact belies a cultural tradition that dates back to the 11th century. The new millennium, therefore, has brought about a renaissance in the city's popularity and reputation.

The city has strong musical connections – Mozart, Rossini, Verdi and Wagner have all performed or staged their works here over the centuries. And the annual calendar of the entire region is still littered with a range of classical, jazz and other music events that are staged in both large, tailor-made venues and in more intimate church settings (see page 104). One of the highlights of the year is the annual opera season from November to June, which is no less revered than those in other Italian cities such as Verona.

In terms of art and architecture, there have been several major contributors to the cultural landscape around the region. The most famous members of the 16th-century Bolognese School of art are the Carracci brothers and Guercino. In the same period the French-born sculptor Giambologna, who went on to make such a mark in Florence, earned his name from his incredible first commission, the Fontana di Nettuno in Piazza Maggiore (see page 69). Much of the area's landscape also owes itself to the great ruling families of the past, such as the Bentivoglio and the d'Este, who commissioned vast palazzi and looming towers to illustrate their importance to lesser citizens. Important artworks are housed together in the Pinacoteca Nazionale, but, as in most of Italy,

● *Piazza Maggiore often vibrates with the sound of a music festival*

the majority of art treasures are still to be found in churches and cathedrals.

In terms of literature, Bologna has never witnessed a great outpouring of prose or poetry as has, say, Florence or Venice, although nearby Ravenna is the burial place of Italy's greatest literary Titan, Dante, after he was banned from Florence (see page 127). The city's best-known modern-day author is Umberto Eco, whose acclaimed works include *The Name of the Rose* (1983) (later a successful film) and *Foucault's Pendulum* (1989).

GIORGIO MORANDI (1890–1964)
A GREAT 20TH-CENTURY ARTIST

Morandi was born in Bologna and spent most of his life painting there or in the village of Vergato 40 km (25 miles) from the city. His landscapes have been compared to the work of Cézanne for the recurring presence of similarly angular shapes and soft hues. Painting during a period of immense social upheaval, technological innovation and artistic expression, he was initially drawn towards the work of the Futurists and Cubists. But ultimately he found his peace in more metaphysical painting, aligning himself with the artists Carra and De Chirico. He became the artist of simple everyday things – vases, fruit, windows – discovering them as if for the first time, revealing their hidden depths and imbuing them with an existential significance. He once said, 'Everything is a mystery, ourselves and the most simple, most infinitesimal of things.'

▶ *The Neptune Fountain and the Palazzo del Podesta*

Shopping

Italy, and in particular the northern Italian cities, are famously synonymous with style – and Bologna is no exception. If you have the money for designer gear, or just want to window-shop and soak up the glamour, head for the intersections of Via dell'Indipendenza, Via Uggo Bassi, Via Rizzoli and Via D'Azeglio, off Piazza Maggiore. These four streets are the domain of designer names, including those great Italian giants Versace and Gucci. Via d'Azeglio is also one of the best places in the city for jewellery if you want to flash even more cash.

Italy is well known for its leather goods: handbags, belts and shoes can be good value compared to prices in other countries. The Italian chain of Benetton can also be found all over the city, so this is the place to go for brightly coloured sweaters and T-shirts.

One of the joys of continental Europe is its range of street markets, where you can browse for hours in the sun. Each day in Piazza Maggiore there's a book market, which is a magnet for bookworms. Obviously the majority of the books are in Italian, but you may pick up a few English titles or an antiquarian gem. There are three flea markets of note that sell a variety of bric-a-brac, second-hand clothes and all manner of other goods: the Mercato di Antiquariato on Piazza Santo Stefano (every second weekend except in January, July and August) is good for antiques; alternatively, try the weekend market in the Parco della Montagnola, or the collectors' market – every Thursday – on Via Valdonica.

Bologna is a renowned centre of gastronomy, and all over the city you'll find mouth-watering cakes at *pasticcerie* (pastry shops), local wines at any *enoteca* and fresh bread at a *forno*. As an edible souvenir of your trip, don't forget to pick up some Parma ham and

Parmesan cheese. Modena's balsamic vinegar is considered among the best in the world, so that's also an ideal souvenir, or an excellent gift for friends. There are plenty of food markets, too, which are great for fresh fruit and vegetables and provisions for picnics, as well as simply offering a buzzing, frenetic atmosphere. Mercato Coperto is on Via Ugo Bassi 2 and Mercato Orefici on Via dei Orefici. Both are open daily in the morning.

For a really beautiful and traditional souvenir, head out of the city to Faenza, 50 km (30 miles) southeast of Bologna. The town is known for its faïence ceramics, which took their inspiration from the Iberian pottery of Majorca in the 12th century. Since then, local craftspeople have continued to produce striking plates, tiles and pots in a variety of designs in blue and yellow. A museum in town details the history of the craft, and numerous factories and shops offer the ceramics for sale. Just make sure they pack it well to survive your journey home.

USEFUL SHOPPING PHRASES

What time do the shops open/close?
A che ora aprono/chiudono i negozi?
Ah keh awra ahprawnaw/kewdawnaw ee nehgotsee?

How much is this?
Quant' è?
Kwahnteh?

Can I try this on?
Posso provarlo?
Pawssaw prawvarrlaw?

My size is ...
La mia taglia è ...
Lah meeyah tahlyah eh ...

I'll take this one, thank you
Prenderò questo, grazie
Prehndehroh kwestaw, grahtsyeh

Eating & drinking

It's not for nothing that Bologna's nickname is *La Grassa* ('The Fat'): in a country obsessed with food, Bologna is undoubtedly the grande dame. While art historians marvel at Florence and fashionistas roam the streets of Milan, gastronomes flock here, to dine in restaurants from the most expensive to the most humble, and stock up on local produce from the markets and shops. And it is that local produce that has secured the Bolognese reputation. The whole region has long been an agricultural phenomenon, an ideal landscape for sheep rearing and pig farming, and a fertile region for growing fruit and wheat.

RESTAURANTS

Italy has a bewildering number of words for its restaurants, but each one should indicate the kind of atmosphere and food to expect if you follow these basic guidelines: an *osteria* is a very simple, basic establishment, not dissimilar to a pub, serving rustic-style food. A *trattoria* is a step up from this, usually family run, and again serving simple dishes such as pasta. A *vineria* is for wine only, although snacks such as olives and nuts may be served, while a *birreria* is predominantly a (beer-)drinking place, but will also serve simple dishes. A *ristorante* is the most formal option, usually complete with tablecloths and full menu. It's usually advisable to book ahead at a

> ### RESTAURANT CATEGORIES
> Price ratings in this book are based on a three-course meal without drinks:
> £ up to €25; ££ between €25 and €40; £££ above €40

ristorante, particularly for an evening meal. Lunch is served between
12.00 and 15.00 and most places do not open in the evening until
20.00, with their kitchens closing at 23.00.

The service charge (*il servizio*) is usually included in the bill
(*il conto*), although it is still considered polite to leave a small tip.

LOCAL SPECIALITIES

Many an American kid must have gone to school with a baloney
sandwich in their lunch pack, but how many would actually have
known that the name is derived from Bologna? In Italy, this spicy
pork sausage, usually served in thin slices, is known as *mortadella*.
Pork is integral to the Bolognese cuisine, unsurprisingly given the
amount of pig farming in the region. Suckling pig has been a delicacy
since the Middle Ages, and the salty cured ham from Parma is
renowned the world over. Pigs' trotters (*zampone*) are also a regular
feature of local menus, although they may be an acquired taste.

The other most famous product of the region is also from Parma.
Parmigiano Reggiano (Parmesan), the hard, cow's-milk cheese, is a
ubiquitous presence on the table of any Italian restaurant around
the globe.

Most regions of Italy proudly claim their right to at least one, but
usually more, pasta shapes, and Bologna is no exception. Tortellini –
tiny pasta balls filled with meat or cheese and served in soups or
with a cream sauce – were purportedly inspired by Venus's navel,
and so proud is the city of its creation that it even has a special
name for a woman who makes them: a *sfoglina*. Tagliatelle, a wide,
ribbon pasta usually served with meat and tomato sauce (*ragù*), also
originates here, as does *pasta verde*, given its pale green colour by
the inclusion of spinach in the pasta dough. *Pasta verde* is often
used for another Bologna staple, lasagne. And who hasn't

reproduced their own version of spaghetti bolognese? In Bologna itself you'll see it listed as *spaghetti al ragù* (spaghetti in meat and tomato sauce).

As for wine, the region is not so well known for its wine production as its neighbour, Tuscany, but it does produce the soft, sweet and slightly sparkling Lambrusco.

USEFUL DINING PHRASES

I would like a table for ... people.
Vorrei un tavolo per ... persone.
Vawrray oon tahvawlaw perr ... perrsawneh.

Waiter/waitress!	**May I have the bill, please?**
Cameriere/cameriera!	Mi dà il conto, per favore?
Cahmehryereh/cahmehryera!	*Mee dah eel cawntaw, perr fahvawreh?*

Could I have it well-cooked/medium/rare please?
Potrei averlo ben cotto/mediamente cotto/poco cotto, per favore?
Pawtray ahvehrlaw behn cawtaw/mehdeeyahmehnteh cawtaw/pawcaw cawtaw perr fahvawreh?

I am a vegetarian. Does this contain meat?
Sono vegetariano/vegetariana (fem.). Contiene carne?
Sawnaw vejetahreeahnaw/vejetahreeahnah. Contyehneh kahrneh?

◀ *An afternoon coffee in the sunshine*

Entertainment & nightlife

Italians are a gregarious lot who like to have fun, and Bologna is one of the most vibrant cities in terms of nightlife and entertainment. The fact that it is also a university town ensures that there's a vibrant mix of young and old, all adding to the atmosphere once the sun goes down. Be warned, however: Bologna is not a cheap city, so if you want to join in the fun you'll have to pay for it.

The evening starts to kick off at around 19.00, when the work day has ended and locals indulge in that most enduring of Italian traditions, the *passeggiata*. This is a time to stroll the streets, enjoy a cocktail or two in the innumerable bars (it is estimated that there are more than 200 *osterie* in Bologna, a tradition going back centuries) and catch up on gossip and news. The main centre for this activity is the pedestrianised Via Clavature, with its many outside tables jam-packed with revellers in the summer months.

Once the initial socialising is over, people usually then head to a restaurant for dinner at around 21.00, lingering over the meal for at least a couple of hours. Dinner is an event in itself – Italians hold no sway with an eat-and-run mentality. Then, finally, it's on to another bar for an after-dinner nightcap before heading home, unless you want to welcome in the early hours on a dance floor.

Again, the student fraternity means that there is no shortage of places for you to show off your moves in the city. The area around the university has plenty of nightlife offerings, although most of the more renowned and trendy nightclubs are in the northwest of the city and just outside. Most clubs charge an entrance fee, unless you are a member, of around €10–15, but you will be entitled to at least

---

● *Early evening drinks in the piazza, before the nightlife kicks off*

one free drink in return. Clubbers must be over the age of 18, and you'll usually be asked for some ID. Clubs go in and out of fashion and favour, so the best way to find out where the action is during your visit is to pick up *051* magazine, which is a free pamphlet found in bars and clubs.

🔺 *Tower of the Palazzo Comunale by night*

Bologna is a relatively gay-friendly city, and there are a number of places where activities are decidedly single. Again, check listings for up-to-date information. Do remember, however, that Italy is still very much a macho culture, not to mention religious, and while society is becoming more tolerant and broad-minded, open displays of affection between same-sex couples in the street will not be met with approval.

Bologna has long had a love affair with jazz, and many of the genre's great international names have performed here. Many of the *osterie* will have impromptu jam sessions, but among the most popular and long-standing jazz clubs are Cantina Bentivoglio and Chet Baker (see page 77), named after the well-known American jazz trumpeter.

The Bolognese love theatre too, and there are plenty of venues around the city. Note, though, that almost all productions, even Shakespeare, are performed in Italian, so if you have limited knowledge of the language, you will simply have to enjoy the spectacle.

Like the rest of the world, cinema has taken over as the most popular cultural activity to enjoy on a regular basis. Italian cinema has long been a thriving industry and its output regularly wins international awards, but if you're hankering after a Hollywood blockbuster there are some cinemas in town that screen films in English.

There are free local multilingual newspapers, available from the tourist office, that also have listings to find out what's going on – *CityBologna*, *BolognaBologna* and *Leggo Bologna*. The tourist board's website ⓦ www.comune.bologna.it is updated frequently but is in Italian only.

Sport & relaxation

Football (*il calcio*) is the national passion in Italy and, as Bologna's team is in the premier league, Serie A, the city is addicted – in season matches are often screened in bars. But the city also offers plenty of other sporting options, both spectator and participatory.

SPECTATOR SPORTS

Football is played at the Stadio R Dall'Ara, which was built in 1927 as one of Italy's first modern sports stadiums. Matches, however, usually sell out way in advance, so if you want to see the action you'll need to plan very well ahead.

Stadio R Dall'Ara ⓐ Via A Costa 174 ⓣ 611 1125 ⓥ Bus 14, 21

Pallacanestro (basketball) is the second most closely followed sport in the city, and Bologna's two teams, Kinder Virtus and Fortitudo, are among the best in Europe. Buy tickets at the Pala Malaguti stadium a couple of hours before the game.

PalaMalaguti ⓐ Via Cervia 1 ⓣ 758 758

PARTICIPATION SPORTS

There are several golf courses outside of Bologna, the best of which is the 18-hole Golf Club Bologna, 8 km (5 miles) south of Bologna. Playing a round will cost around €30 but the advantage is that you don't need to be a member.

Golf Club Bologna ⓐ Via Sabattini 69 in Monte San Pietro ⓣ 969 100 ⓦ www.golfclubbologna.it ⓛ Closed Mondays

Around Bologna are numerous beautiful national parks notable for their interesting geology and varied flora and fauna, including many birds of prey. They also contain hiking and biking trails and have bike hire facilities. Contact the tourist office (see page 150) for information on the following parks: Parco dell'Alto Apennino Modenese, which is a great place to spot eagles, Parco del Delta del Po, with 60 hectares of marshland and lagoons, ideal for bird-watching, Parco del Sassi di Rocca Malatina, known for its peregrine falcons, and Parco dello Stirone with its awesome canyons.

Hiking trails are mapped out in red in the hills surrounding the city. Obtain maps and the latest information from the tourist office or the CAI (Club Alpino Italiano). For avid walkers, the GEA (Grande Escursione Appenninica) is a 400-km (250-mile) trail that traces the Apennine mountain range from Liguria to Le Marche.
Club Alpino Italiano ⊙ 234 856 ⊚ www.cai.it

The Apennines reach heights of 2,000 m (6,560 ft), and usually guarantee good snowfall in winter. There are over twenty ski resorts in the vicinity. Try **Corno alle Scale/Budiara/Val Carlina** (80 km [50 miles] from Bologna, accessible by train from Porretta), **Fiumalbo/Monte Cimone** (take the train from Pistoia), or **Sestola** (67 km [40 miles] from Modena, accessible by train from Porretta).

Bologna has 15 swimming pools, the most central of which are **Stadio** and **Sterlino**. Pool hours are generally 09.30–19.00, but it is worth telephoning ahead to check.
Stadio ⊙ Via dello Sporto 174 ⊙ 615 2520 ⊙ Bus 20
Sterlino ⊙ Via Murri 113 ⊙ 623 7034 ⊙ Bus 13, 20

There are indoor and outdoor clay tennis courts at the **Centro Sportivo Record** ⊙ Via Pilastro 8 ⊙ 503 311 and at the Centro Tennis Padovani ⊙ Via Marzabotto 24 ⊙ 563 127

Accommodation

As a major commercial centre, Bologna has a good supply of hotel rooms. However, during the trade fair seasons of March to early May and September to December, as well as around Christmas, New Year, Easter and the Festa di San Luca (see page 10), accommodation is not only fairly scarce but also considerably more expensive than at other times of the year. Year-round, indeed, Bologna is not a cheap destination, and the range of budget options is far less than in, say, Florence or Rome. Needless to say, the closer you are to the centre, the more you'll pay.

HOTELS

Centrale £ A former aristocrat's home, the Centrale is the best budget option. The rooms are spacious and those on the third floor (no lift) have good views of the Due Torri (Two Towers) and the city.
🅐 Between Via Ugo Bassi and Piazza Roosevelt 🕓 235 162 🚍 Bus 14, 17, 18, 19, 25, 28, 86, B

Marconi £ Recently refurbished, the Marconi offers no-frills basic, clean rooms, some with private baths. It is on a main road, however, so if traffic bothers you, ask for a room at the back.
🅐 Via Marconi 18 🕓 262 832 🖷 235 041 🚍 Bus 11, 17, 21, 25, 28, 30, 36, 38, 39, E

> ### PRICE RATINGS
> The ratings in this book are for a double room for one night (excluding VAT and breakfast).
> **£** Up to €80   **££** Between €80–€150   **££** Over €150

Pallone £ Not far from Piazza Maggiore, the Pallone is one of the best bets if you're on a shoestring budget. The rooms are clean but basic – they each have a washbasin, but baths and showers are communal. ⓐ Via del Pallone 4 ⓣ 421 0533 ⓦ www.albergopallone.it ⓝ Bus 20, 28, 36, 37, 89, 93, 94, 99

Panorama £ Centrally located, not far from Piazza Maggiore, this hostel offers a range of accommodation, from three- to four-bedded dormitory rooms to ordinary doubles, and shared bath facilities. ⓐ Via Livraghi 1 (no sign), off Via Ugo Bassi ⓣ 221 802 ⓦ www.hotelpanoramabologna.it ⓝ Bus 25

Rossini £ Southeast of Piazza G Verdi in the university quarter. Comfortable basic rooms, some with private baths. ⓐ Via Bibbiena 11 ⓣ 237 716 ⓕ 268 035 ⓝ Bus 14, 19, 25, 27, C

Arcoveggio £–££ A friendly and welcoming place to stay only 15 minutes from the historic centre, with very modern rooms, most of which include free WiFi connections. Breakfast is included, and there's the added advantage of on-site parking for a minimal charge. ⓐ Via Lionello Spada 27 ⓣ 355 436 ⓕ 363 102 ⓦ www.hotelarcoveggio.it ⓝ Bus 27

Relais Sante Vincenzi £–££ Housed in a lovely 19th-century building in the heart of the city centre, this charming bed and breakfast has five rooms decorated in bright colours and all with en-suite bathrooms. An American-style breakfast is served at a communal table in the kitchen. ⓐ Via Sante Vincenzi 18 ⓣ 340 757 or 335 610 7993 ⓦ www.relaissantevincenzi.it ⓝ Bus 37 ① Lower rates offered for stays of longer than one week

Tuscolano £–££ Just 5 km (3 miles) northeast of Bologna, the Tuscolano offers the opportunity to sightsee all day then return to a genuine Italian community at night and eat in the local cafés and restaurants. All rooms have private bathrooms and there is on-site parking. Closed August. ⓐ Via del Tuscolano 29 ⓣ 321 024 ⓕ 327 960 ⓦ www.hoteltuscolano.it Ⓝ Bus 27

⬤ *A room at the elegant Hotel Arcoveggio*

Beatrice Bed & Breakfast ££ There are only two rooms here, but each is exquisitely decorated and you certainly get personal service – continental breakfast is served in your room. Shared bathroom. ⓐ Via Indipendenza 56 ⓣ 246 016 ⓕ 421 6296 ⓦ www.bb-beatrice.com ⓝ Bus A, C, 11, 20

Garisenda ££ Rooms are on the third floor of a former palazzo so offer superb views of the two towers (see page 64). Clean and friendly. No lift. ⓐ Via Rizzoli 9, Galeria del Leone 1 ⓣ 224 369 ⓕ 221 007 ⓝ Bus 13, 14, 19, 25, 27

Porta San Mamolo ££ A stylish and romantic option, just off Piazza Maggiore and close to the Due Torri. Some rooms have terraces overlooking the lovely garden, while those on the top floor benefit from a panorama of the entire city. Breakfast included. ⓐ Vicolo del Falcone 6–8 ⓣ 583 056 ⓕ 331 739 ⓝ Bus 32/33 to the Porta San Mamolo stop

Hotel Cavour ££–£££ One of Bologna's best-known and long-standing hotels in a very central location. ⓐ Via Giota 4 ⓣ 228 111 ⓕ 222 978 ⓝ Bus A, C, 11, 20

Hotel Orologio ££–£££ A small, charming hotel that affords views of all the action in Piazza Maggiore. The rooms are elegant and comfortable and breakfast is included. ⓐ Via IV Novembre 10 ⓣ 231 253 ⓕ 260 552 ⓦ www.bolognaho.net ⓝ Bus A, B, 11, 17, 18, 20

Al Cappello Rosso £££ Probably the most romantic and luxurious place to stay in Bologna, right by Piazza Maggiore. The building

dates from 1375 and the red hat (*cappello rosso*) of its name refers to the headgear of the medieval tradesmen who stayed here.
🅐 Via de'Fusari 9 🕿 261 891 🚍 Bus A, B, D, E, 30

Grand Hotel Baglioni £££ You'll want for nothing here, from the free WiFi and satellite TV in all the rooms, to the 24-hour concierge service, parking, personal shopper, shuttle service, tour guide and, for those who really want to show off, the option of your own personal butler. The hotel's restaurant is decorated with 16th-century frescoes, while the food itself is mouth-watering. 🅐 Via Indipendenza 8 🕿 225 445 🖷 234 840 🌐 www.baglionihotels.com
🚍 Bus A, C, 11, 20, 27, 28

HOSTELS

It is compulsory to have either an AIG or AICS card for hostels in Bologna. AICS cards can be purchased directly at the hostels. To get an AIG card in Bologna go to 🅐 Via dell'Unione 6a 🕿 224 913 🖷 224 913 📧 aig_bo@iperbole.bologna.it

Centro Europa Uno £ Eight rooms, two bathrooms, eight showers, a car park and a campsite, located 7 km (4½ miles) from the city centre. 🅐 Via Emilia 297 🕿 625 8352 📧 centroeuropauno@hotmail.com 🚍 Bus 10 ⓘ No credit cards

San Sisto Due Torri £ A modern if bland hostel 6 km (4 miles) from the city centre. If you're dining out in the city, remember that you'll need to be back by 23.30 if you want your room for the night.
🅐 Via Viadagola 5 🕿 501 810 🖷 501 810 📧 hostelbologna@hotmail.com 🚍 Bus 93 & 20 daytime, 21b evening & 301 Sundays ⓘ No credit cards

CAMPING

Centro Turistico Città di Bologna £–££ Located 20 km (12 miles) outside the city, the site consists of bungalows, chalets (both of which have en-suite facilities) and pitches for tents, as well as a swimming pool, snack bar, playground and internet centre.

ⓐ Via Romita 12–4a ⓣ 325 016 ⓕ 325 318 ⓦ www.hotelcamping.com ⓝ Bus 68 stops in front of the reception area

🔺 *The swimming pool at the Centro Turistico campsite*

THE BEST OF BOLOGNA

The *centro storico* (historic centre) is the obvious destination if you only have a short time in Bologna. It's very compact and well preserved, and there's no traffic as the area is pedestrianised. The medieval architecture of the ochre-coloured porticoes, built high enough to accommodate people on horseback, makes a vivid impression.

TOP 10 ATTRACTIONS

- **Piazza Maggiore and La Fontana del Nettuno** The magnificent centrepiece of this grand city exerts a magnetic pull on visitors (see page 68–9).

- **Basilica di San Petronio** One of the largest churches in Christendom, it has a spectacular frescoed interior (see page 62).

- **Due Torri** (Two Towers) Torre degli Asinelli & Torre Garisenda were two of the towers erected by the powerful to impress (see page 64).

- **Portico di San Luca** The finest portico in the city, with 666 arches and 15 chapels (see page 70).

- **San Giacomo Maggiore and l'Oratoria di Santa Cecilia** Bologna's most elegant works of art (see page 70).

- **Palazzo Poggi and the university museums** A wealth of knowledge in a grand setting (see page 86).

- **Orto Botanico** One of the oldest botanical gardens in the world, established in the 16th century (see page 82).

- **Museo Ducati** Track the story of the famous motorbike (see page 49).

- **Museo Morandi** Houses the largest collection of works by Bologna's best-loved modern artist (see page 72).

- **Museo Ebraico** Traces the turbulent history of Jews in Bologna (see page 86).

◆ *Relax in Piazza Maggiore*

Your at-a-glance guide to getting to know Bologna, depending on the time you have available. Walking the ancient streets is probably the easiest way to get the best out of the city.

HALF-DAY: BOLOGNA IN A HURRY

Soak up the lively atmosphere of **Piazza Maggiore**, admire the majestic **Fontana di Nettuno** (see page 69) then relish the quiet of the Gothic **Basilica di San Petronino** with its stunning altar, paintings and frescoes.

Difficult to miss are Bologna's best-known landmarks, the **Due Torri** (Two Towers): **Torre degli Asinelli** and **Torre della Garisenda**. In the 12th century, Bologna had dozens of towers as status symbols – the more powerful the family was that commissioned them, the taller they built the tower. All except these two were torn down in a 19th-century regeneration programme. The Torre degli Asinelli, built between 1109 and 1119, is 97 m (318 ft) high and has an inclination of 2.23 m (over 7 ft). The reward for walking up its 497 steps is breathtaking panoramic views over city rooftops. The Torre della Garisenda was built in the same period as the Asinelli. It is shorter, at 48 m (157 ft) high, but its inclination is 3.22 m (over 10 ft). This tower is closed to the public.

1 DAY: TIME TO SEE A LITTLE MORE

Don't miss the church of **San Giacomo Maggiore**, which was the parish church of the wealthy Bentivoglio family, and now renowned for its 15th-century frescoes in the chapel. The **Oratorio di Santa Cecilia** is also noteworthy for its frescoes illustrating the life of the saint. While admiring all the porticoes in the city, don't fail to pop over to look at the **Portico di San Luca**, stretching 4 km (2½ miles) up the **Colle della Guardia** and including 666 arches and 15 chapels.

2–3 DAYS: SHORT CITY-BREAK

A few more days gives you time to enjoy some of the city's many museums, such as the **Museo Ducati** and factory where the famous motorcycles – the equivalent of a Ferrari on two wheels – are made and exhibited. Also worth visiting are the **Museo Morandi** with over 200 works by Giorgio Morandi, Bologna's most famous contemporary artist, and the **Museo Ebraico**, which explores Jewish history in the region over the course of the last 4,000 years.

Bologna has a total of 21 university museums, but you're unlikely to have either the time or inclination for all of them. Among the most interesting are the **Carducci** room, where the Italian poet Giosue Carducci held his lessons, the **Giovan Antonio Galli Obstetrical Museum** with anatomical plates in wax, clay models and surgical instruments designed by Dr Galli to instruct midwives and surgeons in the art of childbirth, and the **Museo Aldovrandi**, which houses collections by the great Renaissance naturalist Ulisse Aldovrandi, who made Bologna an important centre for the study of botany, zoology and entomology. The University's **Orto Botanico** (Botanical Garden), one of the oldest in the world, has over 100,000 dried plants on display. The grounds are ablaze with hundred of varieties of Mediterranean flora.

LONGER: ENJOYING THE AREA TO THE FULL

With a little longer to explore, follow the **Portico di San Luca** right up into the hills to visit the **Santuario di San Luca**, as well as taking in the panoramic views from here of the city down below. Bologna is also an excellent starting point for trips to Parma (see page 106), famous for its cheese and ham, Ferrara (see page 130), with its palazzos and cultural attractions, and Ravenna (see page 120), with its extraordinary Byzantine mosaics.

Something for nothing

While no one could argue that Bologna is a cheap destination, the great advantage of its historic centre is that its streets are made for walking. Simply strolling through the piazzas and porticoes, offers enough delights to occupy a whole morning, or even a whole day, while spending very little. No visitor will want to miss the magnificent **Piazza Maggiore**, the adjoining **Piazza Nettuno** and the fabulous **Fontana del Nettuno** (see page 69). The great Bolognese churches, in particular **San Petronio** (see page 62) and **San Giacomo Maggiore** (see page 70), with their wonderful artworks, also offer a peaceful respite from the streets outside. The cathedral, too, is worth a visit: the **Metropolitana di San Pietro** (see page 66) houses an *Annunciation* by Ludovico Carracci (1555–1619), founder of the Bolognese School of painting.

Housed within the 16th-century Palazzo, the **Museo di Anatomia Umana** (Museum of Human Anatomy) might seem like a rather macabre place to visit, but it would be a shame to leave Bologna without seeing the waxworks. Models of various parts of the human body, all hand-sculpted, were used until the 19th century for medical demonstrations and instruction, and are so artistically skilled and accurate that they have a strangely appealing quality. ⓐ Via Zamboni 33 ⓘ 372 727 ⓛ 10.00–14.00 daily

One of the nicest walks in the city is from Via Saragozza to Via San Luca on the **Monte della Guardia**, where the **Santuario della Madonna di San Luca** is located, at the end of the **Portico di San Luca**. Not only is it an opportunity to visit this revered pilgrimage site, but the views from here are spectacular and are free to enjoy. The walk takes time and is strenuous in places but is well worth the effort.

Bologna is a sophisticated city, where designer names abound: it doesn't cost anything to window shop and to dream. Among the trendsetters are Furla on Via D'Azeglio, Prada and Salvatore Feragamo on Via Farini, MaxMara and Stefanel on Via Rizzoli, and Gucci, Versace and Emporio Armani in Galeria Cavour.

⏷ *You can stroll all day through the medival streets*

When it rains

The northern Italian climate, while mild, is not immune to a little rainfall every now and then, particularly if you are visiting in low season. But this need not put an end to your enjoyment of the city – much of Bologna's unmissable treasures are found in museums, churches – and even underground.

⬤ *Take shelter in one of the many beautiful churches*

La Casa di Giosue Carducci (House of the Poet Giosuè Carducci) was a former 16th-century church. It was deconsecrated in 1798, and in 1890 became home to the great Tuscan poet Giosuè Carducci (1835–1907), whose works were often seen as a rallying cry for the Unification of Italy. Following his death, one of his most ardent fans, Queen Margherita of Savoy, bought the house in order to preserve the writer's artifacts and possessions, and it has operated as a museum since the 1920s. Among the items on display are Carducci's original desk and writing equipment, as well as a vast library. Since 1990 this has also been the home of the Museo Civico del Risorgimento, exploring the run-up to and the final Unification of the Italian states in 1860 (see page 17). ⓐ Piazza Carducci ⓣ 225 583/347 592 ⓛ 09.00–13.00 Tues–Sun, 09.00–17.00 Thur; admission charge ⓞ Bus 14, 34, 89, 99

Museo Ducati, in the grounds of the company that first produced the legendary Ducati motorcycle in 1946, displays bikes through the decades, as well as their success in racing championships and iconic images of some of their more famous riders. ⓐ Via Ducati 3 ⓣ 641 3343 ⓦ www.ducati.com ⓛ guided tours 11.00 & 16.00 Mon–Fri.

A rainy day will give you the ideal chance to to see a totally different and hidden aspect of the city's history. Among the highlights of an underground tour are the **Bagni di Mario** (Mario's Baths), the elaborately decorated 16th-century cistern that, among other things, supplied water for the **Fontana del Nettuno**, and the **Torrente Aposa** (Aposa Torrent), a 1st-century BC network of tunnels that are the source of centuries of historic trivia. Access is by tour guide only and booking is essential.

Contact a Bologna tour guide ⓣ 467 598 ⓦ www.bolognatourguide.com or the Associazione Amici delle Asque e dei Sotterranei di Bologna ⓣ 522 401

On arrival

TIME DIFFERENCES

Italy is on Central European Time (CET). During Daylight Savings
Time (late Mar–late Oct), clocks are set ahead one hour. When it is
12.00 noon in Italy, it is 11.00 in London, 06.00 in New York, 04.00 in
San Francisco, 20.00 in Sydney, 12.00 midnight in Wellington and the
same time in Johannesburg.

ARRIVING
By air
Marconi International Airport (☎ 647 9615 🌐 www.bologna-airport.it)
is the main airport serving Bologna and is located 6 km (4 miles)
northwest of the city centre. All arrivals come into Terminal A. On
departure all European and domestic services leave from Terminal A
while intercontinental flights leave from Terminal B. The airport has
money-changing facilities, a bank, restaurant and shops. The tourist
information desk, serviced by English-speaking staff, is located in
the centre of the arrivals terminal.

    Aerobus (☎ 290 290 🌐 www.atc.bo.it), the city's airport link,
has a shuttle service that runs in a loop stopping at both terminals,
then at the following stops in the city centre: Ospedale Maggiore,
Via Ugo Bassi, Via Indipendenza/San Pietro, Via Indipendenza/
Arena del Sole and the FS Stazione Centrale. Buses run every
15 minutes between 08.00 and 20.00, and tickets (currently €4.50
one way) can be purchased on board. It's the most cost-efficient way
of getting to and from the airport and the city, but traffic can be
appalling, particularly during rush hour, so the journey can take
about an hour. There is also a *servizio diretto* (direct link) that runs
from the airport to the Fiera district during trade shows. If driving

to the airport yourself, be aware that parking spaces are severely limited.

Forlì Airport (☎ 474 990 ⓦ www.forli-airport.it), located 60 km (40 miles) from Bologna, is the airport of choice for the low-cost airlines, but access is not easy. To get to Bologna city centre it is necessary to take a 15-minute bus or taxi ride into Forlì proper and get a train from there (services every 30 minutes) to the Stazione Centrale. The journey takes 40 minutes and costs €3 one way. A slower option is to take the direct bus service to the bus station on Piazza XX Settembre that is scheduled to coincide with incoming

◆ *An aerial view with the Palazzo Comunale in the foreground*

flights from London, leaving 30 minutes after each arrival. The trip takes 1 hour and 15 minutes and costs €10 per person each way. For the return, the direct bus leaves from the bus station at Piazza XX Settembre once a day at 12.30 Mon–Fri, 15.20 on Sat and 13.15 on Sun (pay the driver on board). If your return flights don't fit in with this schedule, you will have to resort to the train.

By bus

National Express (ⓦ www.nationalexpress.com) operates a service from London Victoria to Bologna for the most budget-restricted traveller. The trip takes more than 24 hours, including stops in Paris and Milan. With low-cost airlines now serving the city, this is only an option for those who positively prefer travelling by road. Bologna's main bus station, the Autostazione (ⓘ 290 290 ⓦ www.autostazionebo.it), is near the mainline station at Piazza XX Settembre.

By car

The *autostrada* approaching Bologna skirts around the city to the north in a ring road, the *tangenziale*, which connects to the major routes. Bologna is linked by the A1 to Milan (2 hours), Florence (1 hour) and Rome (3 hours), by the A13 to Venice and Padua, and by the A14 to Rimini, Ravenna and the Adriatic coast. All motorways in Italy charge tolls, so if you want to avoid these costs (approximately €15 from Rome to Bologna, for example) opt for the *strade statali* (state roads) or SS, which are toll free. Within the *tangenziale* the state roads leading into Bologna connect up to an inner ring road around the city centre. Since the centre is closed to traffic, you will be routed around it on the ring of boulevards that follow the course of the demolished city walls.

By rail

Bologna is a major hub for the FS (Ferrovie dello Stato) rail network, with frequent fast connections to Venice, Florence, Milan, Ravenna, Rimini and almost anywhere else in Italy from the Stazione Centrale (Central Station) on the north side of the city centre, about a 15-minute walk up Via Indipendenza to Piazza Maggiore. If you're carrying heavy luggage, however, and don't want to walk, bus numbers 10, 25 or 30 also take you into the centre – purchase a ticket from *tabaccherie* (tobacconists), newsstands or ticket machines. The Italian State Railway, Trenitalia, is one of the most economical in Europe, with fares in both directions charged by the kilometre.

ⓘ Note that no ticket is valid until it has been stamped, before boarding, in one of the yellow machines on the platform. You might face on-board fines if the ticket is unvalidated.

Stazione Centrale ⓐ Piazza Medaglie d'Oro ⓣ 639 1311

Trenitalia ⓣ 800 915 030 0700 or 1930 from within Italy

ⓦ www.trenitalia.com

FINDING YOUR FEET

It can't be said too many times, the best way to see Bologna is on foot. This way you can marvel at the ingenuity that went into the building of the 70 km (45 miles) of porticoes, the churches, the university and the palazzos. Early in the morning is the optimal time of day for immersing yourself in Bologna's centuries of history. In the evening, after a day spent walking, garner an outside seat at a local *osteria* and absorb the vibrant nightlife around you.

ORIENTATION

The heart of Bologna is its Roman core, Piazza Maggiore, at the junction of the city's two main roads, Via Ugo Bassi and Via Rizzoli. These roads

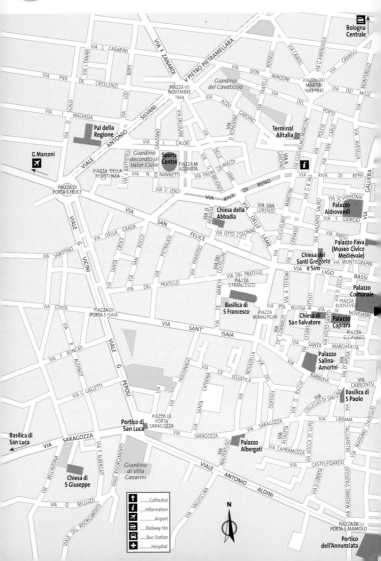

Bologna

0   150 metres
0   150 yards

Parco della Montagnola

Chiesa della Madonna del Soccorso

PIAZZA DI PORTA MASCARELLA

Palazzina della Viola

Museo di Fisica

Orto Botanico

Pinacoteca Nazionale

Nuovo Palazzo Bentivoglio

Museo di Geologia e Paleontologia

Basilica di S Martino

Palazzo Grassi

Palazzo Poggi

Metropolitana di San Pietro

San Giacomo Maggiore

Due Torri

Palazzo Malvezzi de' Medici

Chiesa di San Bartolomeo

Palazzo Fantuzzi

Stazione S Vitale

Palazzo del Podestà

Museo Civico Archeologico

Casa Pepoli

Palazzo Pepoli Campogrande

Palazzo dell'Archiginnasio

Abbazia di Santa Stefano

Chiesa di San Giovanni in Monte

Palazzo Davia Bargellini

Chiesa di Santa Maria dei Servi

Palazzo Hercolani

Aula Magna Room

Palazzo Zani

Basilica di San Domenico

Eleonora Duse Theatre

Palazzo Vizzani

Palazzo Pini

Casa di Giosuè Carducci

Palazzo Ruini

Chiesa della Madonna del Baraccano

are the new face of the old Via Emilia, which at one time traversed the entire region. The area now called the *centro storico* (historic centre) is ringed by the *circonvallazione*, the busy perimeter road that follows the demarcation of the old city walls, joining up at the 12 city gates.

GETTING AROUND
Public transport
Take advantage of the city's efficient local bus system, the ATC. Before boarding any bus you must purchase a ticket at a tobacconist's, the tourist office (see page 151) or the main bus station at Piazza XX Settembre, at the booth outside the railway station on Piazza Medaglie d'Oro, in the centre at Via IV Novembre 16, or at Piazza Re Enzo on Via Rizzoli. Tickets are valid for one hour, on as many buses as you want, but, as with trains, you must validate them by using the punching machine when you get on board. If you

---

IF YOU GET LOST, TRY …

Excuse me, do you speak English?
Mi scusi, parla inglese?
Mee scoozee, parrla eenglehzeh?

Excuse me, is this the right way to the old town/the city centre/the tourist office/the station/the bus station?
Mi scusi, è questa la strada per la città vecchia/al centro città/l'ufficio informazioni turistiche/alla stazione ferroviario/alla stazione degli autobus?
Mee scoozee, eh kwehstah lah strahda perr lah cheetta vehkyah/ahl chentraw cheetteh/looffeechaw eenforrmahtsyawnee tooreesteekeh/ahlla stahtsyawneh ferrawvyaryo/ahlla stahtsyawneh delee ahootawboos?

---

plan to make frequent use of the bus service, purchase a CityPass, which costs around €6.50 and is valid for eight journeys. ATC
☎ 290 290 ⓦ www.atc.bo.it

Taxis
At Marconi International, the taxi rank is outside Terminal A. The journey usually costs between €15–20, depending on traffic, which is usually heavy. The price can be higher if you have a substantial amount of luggage.

Car hire
Unless it's absolutely necessary, you should avoid driving in Bologna – cars are restricted in the city centre, and for the most part parking is nonexistent. If you must drive, the following companies have offices at at least one of the airports and in Bologna proper, mostly along the northern end of Via Marconi/Via Amendola. If you're planning to tour around the region it's usually more economical to book a fly/drive package from your home country.

Before leaving the car park, make sure you have all necessary documentation and that you know how to operate the vehicle. Remember to drive on the right-hand side of the road.

AutoEurope ⓦ www.autoeurope.com
Marconi airport ☎ 1 888 223 5555 🕐 08.00–23.00 Mon–Sun;
Bologna ⓐ 12-F Via Amendola ☎ 1 888 223 5555

Avis ⓦ www.avis.com
Forli airport ☎ 0543 781835; Marconi airport ☎ 647 2032;
Bologna ⓐ Via Le Pietrammellara 27-D ☎ 255 024;
ⓓ Via Marco Polo 91 ☎ 634 1632

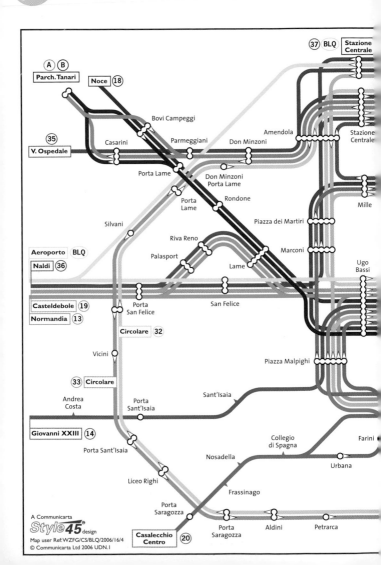

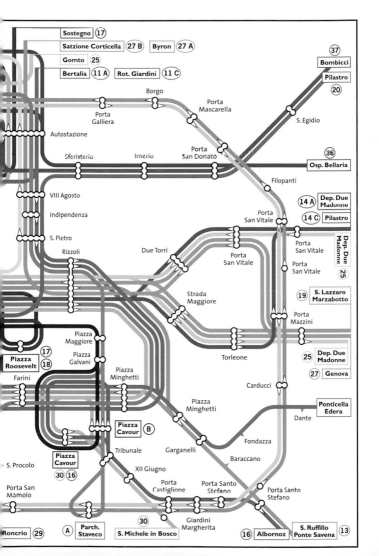

EasyCar Ⓦ www.easycaritalia.it
Forli airport ❶ 0543 473436; Marconi airport ❶ 800 939293

Europcar Ⓦ www.europcar.com
Forli airport ❶ 0543 473241; Marconi airport ❶ 647 2111;
Bologna ⓐ Via Amendola 12 ❶ 247 101

Hertz Ⓦ www.hertz.com
Forli airport ❶ 0543 782637; Marconi airport ❶ 647 2015;
Bologna ⓐ Via Amendola 16 ❶ 254 830

Sixt Budget Ⓦ www.e-sixt.co.uk
Forli airport ❶ 08701 567 567; Marconi airport ❶ 647 2027;
Bologna ⓐ Via del Lavoro 8-D ❶ 768 261

❿ *Peering through a porthole, Palazzo Malvezzi*

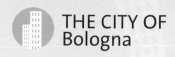

Piazza Maggiore & the Centro Storico

The *centro storico* (historic centre) and the surrounding pedestrianised streets should be any visitor's first port of call. The square, Piazza Maggiore, once the site of the Roman forum, and until the 19th century still the main trading area of the city, remains to this day a bustling cultural centre. At any given time of day you may come across a group of schoolkids kicking a football about, students lounging over their books, or businesspeople stopping for a quick gossip on their way to another meeting. The geographical heart of the city is also its social core.

SIGHTS & ATTRACTIONS

Basilica di San Domenico

The highlight of this 13th-century church is, unsurprisingly, the ornate tomb of San Domenico, crafted by great artists of the day including Nicola Pisano, Guglielmo, Nicola dell'Arca, Alfonso Lombardi and even a young Michelangelo. The latter's *San Procolo* figure decorating the tomb shows clear indications of the artistry that would eventually lead to the creation of *David* and many other masterpieces.

ⓐ Piazza San Domenico 13 ⓣ 640 0411 ⓛ 08.00–13.00 & 15.30–19.30 Mon–Sat; admission free ⓐ Bus 16, 30, 38, 39 A, C

Basilica di San Petronio

The most important church in Bologna, the Basilica di San Petronio is also one of the largest in Christendom. Although it looms over the Piazza Maggiore, the 14th-century façade is sadly unremarkable – rumour has it that when the Vatican heard that there were plans to

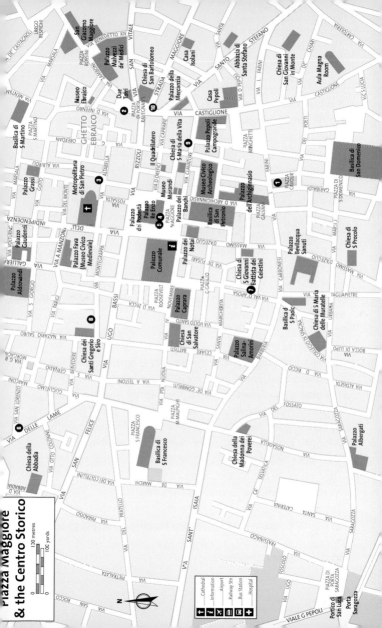

Piazza Maggiore & the Centro Storico

0   100 metres
0   100 yards

N

Cathedral
Information
Airport
Railway Stn
Bus Station
Hospital

LARGO RESPIGHI
VIALE DE CASTIGLIA
VIA DE' CHIARI

San Giacomo Maggiore
Palazzo Malvezzi de' Medici
PIAZZA ROSSINI
VIA MARSALA
VIA ZAMBONI
VIA SAN VITALE
VIA SAN DONATO
VIA BENEDETTO XIV
Chiesa di San Bartolomeo
Casa Isolani
Abbazia di Santa Stefano
Chiesa di San Giovanni in Monte
Aula Magna Room
VIA SANTO STEFANO
VIA CASTIGLIONE
Museo Ebraico
Palazzo della Mercanzia
Casa Pepoli
Due Torri ②
PIAZZA DI PORTA RAVEGNANA
STRADA MAGGIORE
⑩
GHETTO EBRAICO
VIA D'INFERNO
PIAZZA SAN MARTINO
Basilica di S Martino
VIA MENTANA
VIA ALTABELLA
VIA RIZZOLI
Il Quadrilatero
VIA CAPRARIE
Chiesa di S Maria della Vita
Palazzo Pepoli Campogrande
⑨
Metropolitana di San Pietro ③
VIA DELL'INDIPENDENZA
Palazzo Grassi
VIA GOITO
VIA OBERDAN
VIA FOSSALTA
VIA ORFEO
Museo Morandi
Museo Civico Archeologico
Palazzo dell'Archiginnasio ①
PIAZZA CAVOUR
VIA FARINI
Basilica di San Domenico
PIAZZA DI SAN DOMENICO
VIA GARIBALDI
Palazzo Gaudenti
VIA DEL MONTE
Palazzo di Podestà
Palazzo Re Enzo
Palazzo dei Banchi
④
PIAZZA MAGGIORE ⑤
Basilica di San Petronio
PIAZZA GALVANI
Palazzo Bevilacqua Sanuti
Chiesa di S Procolo
Palazzo Fava (Museo Civico Medievale)
VIA A MANZONI
VIA MONTEGRAPPA
Palazzo dei Notai
i
VIA D'AZEGLIO
VIA MASSIMO D'AZEGLIO
VIA CARBONESI
Palazzo Aldrovandi
VIA S GIORGIO
VIA GALLIERA
Palazzo Comunale
VIA DE' FUSARI
Chiesa di S Giovanni Battista dei Celestini ⑦
Basilica d S Paolo
Chiesa di S Maria delle Muratelle
VIA TAGLIAPIETRE
VIA URBANA
VIA DE' PEPOLI
VIA DELLE LAME
PIAZZA ROOSEVELT
Palazzo Caprara
VIA IV NOVEMBRE
VIA D'ZECCA
VIA C GALLIERA
PIAZZA MARGHERITA
VIA VAL D'APOSA
VIA DE' GOMBRUTI
VIA BOCCA DI LUPO
VIA D BICCIO
Chiesa dei Santi Gregorio e Siro
Chiesa di San Salvatore
Palazzo Salina-Amorini
VIA BARBERIA
VIA CARDUCCI
VIA NAZARIO SAURO
VIA UGO BASSI
VIA BELVEDERE
VIA G GERVASIO
VIA S NAZARIO SAURO
VIA CESARE BATTISTI
VIA SANTA CHIARA
VIA NOSADELLA
VIA ALTASETA
⑧
⑥
VIA DE MARCHI
VIA DEL PRATELLO
VIA SAN FELICE
VIA OTTO COLONNE
Chiesa della Abbadia
VIA DELL'ABBADIA
VIA SAN ROCCO
VIA SAN LORENZO
VIA MARCONI
VIA GUGLIELMO MARCONI
Basilica di S Francesco
PIAZZA S FRANCESCO
PIAZZA M MALPIGHI
Chiesa della Madonna dei Poveri
VIA SELVATICA
VIA CA' SELVATICA
VIA SANT'ISAIA
VIA DEI COLTELLINI
VIA DE' MARCHI
VIA PARADISO
VIA PIETRALATA
VIA FOSSATO
VIA DEL FOSSATO
VIA SARAGOZZA
Palazzo Albergati
VIA URBANA
VIALE G PEPOLI
PIAZZA DI PORTA SARAGOZZA
Porta Saragozza
Portico di San Luca
VIA SARAGOZZA
VIA TRASSINAGO
VIA FOSCOLO
VIA UGO
VIA CATERINA

make it grander than St Peter's in Rome, they carefully reallocated funds elsewhere and the exterior was never finished.

The interior, however, certainly doesn't disappoint. Among the highlights are the *Madonna and Child* and carvings and bas-reliefs depicting stories of the Old Testament by Jacopo della Quercia, frescoes detailing the life of San Petronio, Bologna's patron saint, and the spectacular *Martyrdom of Saint Sebastian* on the altar by Lorenzo Costa.

In total there are 22 chapels in the basilica, with paintings, sculptures, glasswork and faïence by many Bolognese artists, but the most compelling is the Cappella Bolognini (Bolognini Chapel), financed by the Bolognini family's silk empire, with frescoes by DeModena entitled *The Journey of the Kings*, *Paradise* and *Hell*.
ⓐ Piazza Maggiore ① 225 442 🕐 07.30–13.00 & 15.30–18.30 Mon–Sun; admission free Ⓝ Bus 1, 13, 14, 17, 18, 19, 20, 25 ❶ No bags other than ladies' handbags allowed inside

Due Torri (Two Towers)

These two leaning towers may stand out as beacons today, but in the Middle Ages, when they were built, they were just two of more than 100 such landmarks, built to illustrate the importance and wealth of each noble family that ordered their construction. Others do still exist around the city, but none is as majestic. It's possible to climb the tallest tower, the Torre degli Asinelli, at 96 m (320 ft); if you have a head for heights, this offers some of the finest views over the rooftops of the historic centre. The smaller Torre Garisenda, at 48 m (157 ft), however, is closed to the public.
ⓐ Piazza di Porta Ravegnana 🕐 09.00–19.00 Mon–Sun; admission charge Ⓝ Bus 10, 11, 13, 14, 17, 18, 19, 20, 25, 27, 29, 30, 37, 90, 96

⏵ *The Asinelli and Garisenda towers*

Il Quadrilatero and Il Mercato di Mezzo

To the east of Piazza Maggiore is an area known as Il Quadrilatero (roughly 'the quadrant'), a labyrinthine area of medieval alleyways that ooze with historic atmosphere. From Roman times onwards this was the heart of the trading area of the city, and many of the street names still recall the merchants that plied their wares here: *orefici* (jewellers), *clavature* (locksmiths), *pescherie* (fishmongers), *drapperie* (textile merchants) and more.

The spirit of commerce still fills the air with the daily Mercato di Mezzo, stalls piled high with fresh fruit and vegetables as the traders call out to customers and passers-by advertising their produce. At night, however, a more genteel atmosphere pervades as the lights from the fashionable bars and cafes shine down on their chic clientele.

Ⓝ Bus 13, 14, 19, 25, 27

Metropolitana di San Pietro

It's easy to lose sight of Bologna's cathedral, dwarfed as it is by more recent and more impressive buildings at the heart of the busy Via dell'Indipendenza. But look out for the 13th-century marble lions that grace the entrance and you'll have found your spot.

Inside, too, the building is a bit of a hotch-potch of styles from over the centuries, each one added to repair or replace damage caused by fires or earthquake. Highlights, however, include Ludovico Carracci's *Annunciation* in the sacristy.

The main event in the cathedral each year is during the Festa di San Luca in May, when the icon of the saint is brought here from her hillside shrine, the Santuario della Madonna di San Luca.

ⓐ Via dell'Indipendenza 7 Ⓣ 222 112 Ⓛ 07.30–12.00, 16.00–18.30 Mon–Sun Ⓝ Bus 11, 27, A, C

Palazzo dei Banchi

The Palazzo dei Banchi (Bankers' House), on the eastern side of Piazza Maggiore, is the area in which money-lenders traditionally set up their benches (*banchi*) to do business. The building is most notable for its classical façade, designed by the architect Vignola in the 16th century, and for its elegant arcades, which are still referred to as Il Pavaglione, because the cocoons of the *pava* (silkworm) were sold here during the Middle Ages.

🅐 Piazza Maggiore 🅒 Closed to the public 🅝 Bus 1, 3, 13, 14, 17, 18, 19, 20, 25

Palazzo Comunale

The Palazzo Comunale (town hall) today combines various architectural styles from the 13th to the 15th centuries, as various city dignitaries added to the building. The original structure dates from 1287, but further additions were made in 1365 and again in 1425. The most notable feature of the façade is the statue of Pope Gregory XIII, peering down over the main entrance. Inside, the first floor of the palazzo is now home to various important works of art, most notably in the Sala di Ercole (Hercules' Room) featuring a statue of the eponymous god by Alfonso Lombardi. Among other works here are Ludovico Carracci's *Phaeton's Fall* and the *Madonna and the Earthquake* by Francesco Francia. Paintings and frescoes also adorn the Sala Farnese, with works by the Carracci brothers and Tintoretto, among others.

🅐 Piazza Maggiore 🅣 201 111 🅒 09.30–18.30 Tues–Sat, 10.00–18.30 Sun; admission charge 🅝 Bus 1, 3, 13, 14, 17, 18, 19, 20, 25

Palazzo dei Notai

Tucked neatly between the Basilica di San Petronio and Palazzo Comunale is the modest, Gothic-style Palazzo dei Notai (House of the Notaries), originally dating from the 13th century. For centuries this was home to the Guild of Notaries and where Bologna's residents would come to seek legal advice and representation.

🅐 Piazza Maggiore 🕐 09.00–13.00 Mon & Wed, 15.00–19.00 Tues, Thur & Fri 🚍 Bus 1, 3, 13, 14, 17, 18, 19, 20, 25

Palazzo del Podestà & Palazzo Re Enzo

The corner of Piazza Maggiore and Piazza Nettuno is occupied by these two palazzi, originally dating from the 13th century but much altered over the years. The Palazzo del Podestà, the city's main law court, was entirely renovated in 1484 under the instruction of the influential Giovanni II Bentivoglio, and today only the Arengo Tower, built in 1212, remains of the original structure. The pillars surrounding the tower are decorated with terracotta statues representing the city's eight patron saints, masterfully sculpted by Alfonso Lombardi.

The Palazzo Re Enzo is named after Enzo, illegitimate son of Emperor Frederick II, the 13th-century king of Sicily and Holy Roman Emperor. During one of the continued skirmishes between the papal loyalists (Guelphs) and the supporters of the empire (Ghibellines), the Guelphs defeated Frederick in 1249 and took Enzo as their prisoner. He was incarcerated in this building for 22 years, until his death in 1271, although by all accounts his imprisonment was not too arduous: he led a sybaritic life enhanced by poetry and women, and was tended to by servants.

🅐 Piazza Maggiore 🕐 Both palazzi are closed to the public except during exhibitions 🚍 Bus 1, 3, 13, 14, 17, 18, 19, 20, 25

Piazza Maggiore

The hub of public life in Bologna, Piazza Maggiore exerts an almost magnetic pull to visitors and locals, and inevitably you will start or end up here. The piazza's antechamber, **Piazza Nettuno**, is graced by the exquisite **Fontana del Nettuno** (Fountain of Neptune), designed in 1563 by Tommaso Laureti and embellished with the work of Flernish sculpture Jean de Boulogne (known in Italian as Giambologna). Around Il Gigante, as Neptune is affectionately known, Giambologna also sculpted many putti (cherubs) and mermaids. Very near here, on **Palazzo Comunale**, is another fountain, referred to as **La Fontana Vecchia** (Old Fountain), which was also designed by Tommaso Laureti and is indeed older than the Neptune Fountain.

🔺 *Piazza Maggiore*

Portico di San Luca

At the Porta Saragozza begins the portico to beat all porticoes. Traversing 4 km (2½ miles), all the way up the Colle della Guardia to the Santuario della Madonna di San Luca, and taking in some 666 arches and 15 chapels en route, it has the impressive honour of being the longest continuous arcade in the world. This extraordinary feat of architectural engineering was created by Giovanni Monti, begun in 1674 and completed in 1739. ⊙ Bus 20

San Giacomo Maggiore

It goes at least some way to explaining the vast wealth of the noble families of Bologna in the Middle Ages when you consider that the spectacular San Giacomo Maggiore was the parish church of the Bentivoglio family. It was Giovanni Bentivoglio II who commissioned

● *Portico di San Luca, the longest arcade in the world*

the artist Lorenzo Costa to complete three frescoes in the Bentivoglio Chapel – the *Triumph of Death*, the *Apocalypse* and a *Madonna Enthroned* – surrounding in self-indulgent manner the family tombs. Costa also worked, alongside Francesco Francia and Amico Aspertini, at Giovanni's request, on scenes illustrating the life of Saint Cecilia in the oratory dedicated to the saint.

ⓐ Piazza Rossini, Via Zamboni 15 ☏ 225 970 🕐 07.00–12.00 & 15.00–18.00 Mon–Sun; admission free ⓥ Bus 1, 3, 14, 17, 18, 19, 20, or 25

LA FAMIGLIA BENTIVOGLIO – WARRIORS AND PATRONS

The Bentivoglio family was one of the great warring dynasties of medieval Bologna. Not only did they wield immense political power over the region at a time when Italy was divided into many different states and kingdoms, but they also saw the advancement and procurement of art as a signature of wealth and prestige. At the height of their power in 1460, Sante Bentivoglio sought to set their importance in stone with the building of a large family palazzo on Via Zambone. But it was Sante's son, Giovanni II, who contributed most to the city in terms of art and architecture. During his 46-year reign, Bologna became a hotbed of artistic activity, most notably with the school of Francesco Francia, also known as Francesco Raibolini (1450–1517), and in the buildings around the university quarter, which was the family's stronghold. Times were changing, however – by 1506 Bologna had become a Papal State and Giovanni II was overthrown and exiled. But perhaps through nostalgia or romanticism, the family is still remembered in parts of the city – the famous jazz club on Via Mascarella still bears the influential family name (see page 77).

CULTURE

Museo Civico Archeologico (Archaeological Museum)

Formerly a hospital for the terminally ill, this impressive 14th-century building is now home to an equally impressive collection of archaeological relics. Perhaps not surprisingly, since they were the first civilisation in the region, the highlight of the collection is the Etruscan section, with displays of jewellery, coins and other finds. The Egyptian section, too, is superb, including an eerie gathering of mummies in the basement. Greek and Roman sculpture (copies, not originals) and a section on prehistoric finds complete the experience.

🅐 Via dell'Archiginnasio 2 🅣 233 849 🅛 09.00–18.30 Tues–Sat, 10.00–18.30 Sun; admission charge 🅜 Bus, 11, 13, 14, A, B

Museo Morandi

Giorgio Morandi (1890–1964) is Bologna's best-loved modern artist and this museum is entirely dedicated to his work, with more than 300 paintings on display. Also in the museum is a reconstruction of his study, including his easel, brushes and other tools of his trade.

🅐 Piazza Maggiore 6 🅣 203 332 🅛 09.00–15.00 Tues–Fri, 10.00–18.00 Sat–Sun; admission free

RETAIL THERAPY

Bologna is a shopper's paradise – whatever you are looking for. Food, clothes, antiques and books are among the best buys; every Italian designer has a flagship store here, and the innumerable

🅓 *Museo Civico*

delicatessens, as well as open-air markets, offer a mouthwatering array of Bolognese specialities. The presence of the university also ensures a wide range of bookstores.

Majani Chocoholics beware – enter Majani and you may end up buying their entire stock! This delectable *cioccolataio* has been in this spot since 1796. Via Carbonese 5 234 302 Bus 20, 38, 94, D

Mercato delle Erbe This vast covered market oozes with the sights and aromas of stall upon stall of fresh fruit and vegetables (see page 66). Via Ugo Bassi 2 07.00–13.00 & 17.00–19.00 Mon–Sat, closed Thur & Sat pm Bus 14, 17, 18, 19, 25, 28, 86, B

Paris Texas Italy This is the place to come if you want designer gear from the likes of Dolce & Gabbana and Versace at bargain prices. Via Altabella 11 225 741 09.30–13.00 & 15.00–19.00 Mon–Sun Bus 14, 17, 18, 19, 25, 28, 86, B

Spazio Minghetti The Spazio Minghetti building is almost as important as the stock, with its baroque detailing and statue-filled garden. Inside is interior style with a difference – if you fancy a sofa upholstered in horsehair or some antelope skin rugs, they'll be happy to oblige. Piazza Minghetti 3 265 670 09.30–13.00 & 15.30–20.00 Mon–Sat Bus 20, 29, 30

Tamburini Probably the best food shop in the city – choose from an incredible array of homemade pastas, local hams and cheeses. Via Caprarie 1 234 726 Bus 1, 3, 13, 14, 17, 18, 19, 20, 25

TAKING A BREAK

Bar e Winery £ ❶ Take a break from all that shopping and relax with a glass of wine in this sleek bar. ⓐ Galleria Cavour 1 ❶ 227 048 ❶ 18.00–21.30 Mon–Sun ⓝ Bus 20, 28, A

Due Torri £ ❷ A very central, good-value lunch option, with the added benefit of a range of vegetarian choices. ⓐ Via De' Giudei 6 ❶ lunch only 12.00–15.00 Mon–Sat ⓝ Bus 11, 20, 29, 30 ❶ No credit cards

Faccioli £ ❸ A great place for a pre-dinner drink, in the shadow of one of the city's towers. ⓐ Via Altabella 15b ❶ 18.00 onwards, Mon–Sun. Closed Sat & Sun July & Aug ⓝ Bus 1, 3, 13, 14, 17, 18, 19, 20, 25

La Torinese £ ❹ Anyone with a sweet tooth should make a beeline here – the hot chocolate is quite simply delicious, as are the pastries. ⓐ Piazza Re Enzo 1a ❶ 236 743 ⓝ Bus 11, 20, 29, 30, A

Rosa Rose £ ❺ If your feet are weary from pounding the porticoes, stop off at Rosa Rose for a leisurely cappuccino and ice cream. ⓐ Piazza Re Enzo ⓝ Bus 1, 3, 13, 14, 17, 18, 19, 20, 25

AFTER DARK

Restaurants
San Lorenzo £ ❻ There's nothing chic about this self-service place, but it's a good option for budget-conscious hungry travellers and the dishes are traditionally Bolognese. ⓐ Via San Lorenzo 4 ❶ 11.30–15.00 & 18.30–21.30 Mon–Sun ⓝ Bus 17, 21, D, E

Le Navate Café £–££ ❼ Tucked away on a tiny street near Via Barberia, this friendly trattoria is simple in style but superb in quality and service. ⓐ Via Val D'Aposa 7E ⓣ 262 793 ⓐ 12.00–14.30 & 17.30–20.30 Tues–Sat. Closed Sun ⓝ Bus 30, 39, A

Montegrappa del Nello ££ ❽ The house specialities here include *tortellina Montegrappa* (tortellini served in cream and meat sauce), *graminia* (thin spaghetti served with truffles, mushrooms and cream) and wonderful salads of mushrooms, truffles, Parmesan cheese and artichokes. ⓐ Via Montegrappa 2 ⓣ 236 331 ⓛ 12.00–15.00 & 19.00–23.30 Tues–Sun ⓝ Bus 20, 28, A ⓘ Reservations are recommended

Trattoria Gianni – A la Vecia Bulagna ££ ❾ One of the most traditional dishes on the menu here is *bolliti*, a local meat stew, but there are also a large number of pasta dishes to choose from. The wine list, too, concentrates on the local region. ⓐ Via delle Clavature 18 ⓣ 229 434 ⓛ Closed Mon & Sun ⓝ Bus 11, 20, 29, 30

Ristorante Pappagallo (The Parrot) £££ ❿ If you've got the budget for it, don't miss the opportunity to dine in Bologna's best restaurant, sitting in the shadows of the Due Torri within a 14th-century palazzo. The *lasagna verdi al forno* (baked lasagna with spinach) is a house speciality. ⓐ Piazza della Mercanzia 3C ⓣ 232 807 ⓛ 12.30–14.30 & 19.30–20.30 Mon–Sat. Closed Sun & two weeks in Aug ⓝ Bus 1, 3, 13, 14, 17, 18, 19, 20, 25 ⓘ Reservations recommended

Cinema
The following cinemas screen some films in English:
Adriano English films each Monday. ⓐ Via San Felice 52 ⓣ 555 127 ⓝ Bus 13, 19, 36, 38, 81, 87, 91, 92, 93

Nosadella Films in their original language so US films will be in English. Via Nosadella 331 506 www.nosadella.it Bus 14, 20, 21, 38, 89, 94, E

Tiffany English films each Wednesday. Piazza di Porta Saragozza 5 585 253 Bus 20, 33, 39, 94, D

Gay & lesbian nightlife

Bologna is a relatively gay-friendly city and there are a number of places where activities are decidedly single-sex – again, check listings for up-to-date information. Among the more popular places are:

Cassero Bologna's most famous gay club. Piazza di Porta Lame 649 4416 21.30–02.30 Sun night disco. Thur LesBo (lesbian) night Bus 20, 38, 94, D

Da Renzo e Andrea A popular gay bar. Via L/Spada 28 222 1993 Bus 20, D

Gay Zen Café Frequented by a mixed crowd. Via Mascarella 79 222 1993 Bus 20, D

Jazz clubs

Bologna has long had a love affair with jazz and many of the genre's great international names have performed here. Many of the *osterie* will have impromptu jam sessions, but among the most popular and long-standing jazz clubs are:

Cantina Bentivoglio You can have a drink or dinner here in the old wine cellars of Palazzo Bentivoglio. Via Mascarella 4 265 416

Chet Baker You can dine and listen to live music here also. Via Polese 7 223 795 www.chetbaker.com

The university quarter

As home to the oldest university in Europe, it's not surprising that Bologna is often referred to as *Bologna la Dotta* (Bologna the Learned). The university began life in 1088 as a unique institution – it was the students themselves who set it up and organised its management, including the hiring of lecturers and professors. Its first speciality was the study of law, which laid the foundations for modern legal practice, followed by philosophy and medicine; it became known particularly as a centre for the study of anatomy and astronomy. It was an alumnus of Bologna, Vacarius, who set up the law department of that other great seat of learning, Oxford University, in 1144.

Today the university is still the most respected in Italy. The main area of the university quarter is Via Zamboni, where lively cafés buzz with the chatter of philosophising students. However, the area is known for more than just learning: the city's theatre district is by Piazza Verdi, there's elegant shopping to be done along Via Oberdan and antiques shops along Via San Vitale, while the Ghetto Ebraico (Jewish ghetto) remains an atmospheric area of narrow alleyways and cobbled lanes.

SIGHTS & ATTRACTIONS

Chiesa di San Bartolomeo

This tiny 16th-century church, dwarfed by the Due Torri (see page 64), is rather unprepossessing outside, but its real gem is its interior frescoes, including *San Carlo al sepolcro di Varalla* by Ludovico Carracci, one of Bologna's finest Renaissance artists.

ⓐ Piazza di Porta Ravegnana 🕐 07.00–13.00 & 15.00–16.30
🚌 Bus 14, 19, 27, C

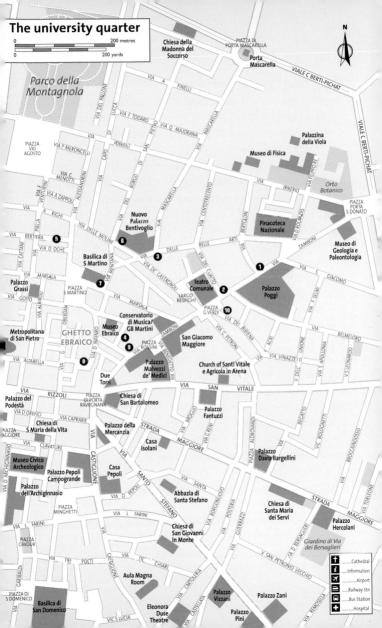

Ghetto Ebraico (Jewish Ghetto)

Bologna's Jewish community was not only tolerated but also respected in the Middle Ages, but the anti-Jewish measures laid down by the papal bull (charter) of 1555 condemned Jews to live in a segregated area, known as a ghetto, and restrict their trades to money-lending and medicine. The Jews remained in these confined conditions, behind elegant Via Rizzoli, until the middle of the 19th century: names of some streets such as Via dell'Inferno (Street of Hell) clearly illustrate how they felt about their life and situation. Some buildings still sport spyholes in the doors, which indicates the suspicion and fear of persecution that afflicted the Jews' everyday lives.

Despite its unhappy past, however, today the area is an atmospheric enclave of narrow alleyways and old buildings, many of which now house excellent restaurants. To learn more about the city's Jewish heritage, visit the Museo Ebraico (see page 86).

Another place in the area that belies its past is the Galleria Acquaderni, an elegant shopping centre that still sports ancient frescoes on some of its walls. In its past life, the building was a church, the Chiesa di San Giobbe, then a much-feared hospital for those suffering from *mal francese* ('French evil' or syphilis).

The area is also home to many of the medieval towers constructed by wealthy families at the time: the Torre degli Uguzzoni in Vicolo Tubertini, the 11th-century Torre Prendiparti in Via Sant'Alo, Casa-torre Guidozagni near Via Albriroli, and the Torre degli Azzoguidi on Via Caduti di Cefalonia.

ⓐ Ghetto Ebraico Ⓝ Bus 11, 13, 14, 19, C

◗ *Wander the alleyways of the Ghetto Ebraico*

Nuovo Palazzo Bentivoglio

The Bentivoglio family was the most powerful in Bologna in the Middle Ages, but by the end of the 15th century the tide had turned, and in 1507 their grand palace was pulled down by less subservient citizens. Perhaps through guilt, or perhaps through realising there was a value in history, this new palazzo was then built a few years later in their honour. Today it is home to private residences and offices, but visitors can take a look at the courtyard with its lovely Romanesque loggias.

ⓐ Via delle Belle Arti 8 Ⓝ Bus 20, 28, 36, 37, C

Orto Botanico

Bologna's Orto Botanico (Botanical Gardens) were first established in 1568, making them one of the oldest such institutions in Europe; their popularity has never waned. The plants were initially intended to assist medical students at the nearby university, and to explore the healing qualities of different species. Today there are ornamental gardens, greenhouses filled with exotic plants from around the world, a woodland park and a man-made pond breeding lilies and other wetland plants. Without question, spring is the best time to visit, when the plants are a riot of colour.

ⓐ Via Irnerio 42 Ⓣ 209 1299 Ⓛ 08.00–15.00 Mon–Fri, 08.30–midday Sat

Piazza VIII Agosto

Unless you're a real history buff, there's nothing – in the early part of the week – to draw you to this square (which takes its name from the date the Bolognese defeated the Austrians in the First War of Italian Independence in 1848). But on Fridays and Saturdays it becomes a bustling, colourful marketplace attracting anyone and everyone in Bologna, in search of bargain books, leather goods, china and a whole host of other paraphernalia. A sister market is held up the steps in Giardini della Montagnola.

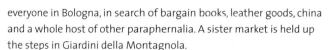 Piazza VIII Agosto Bus 20, 28, 36, 37, 89, 93, 94, 99

Teatro Comunale

Built on the site of the former Bentivoglio Palace by Antonio Bibiena in 1763, this theatre has been entertaining the Bolognese for more than three centuries. Although the present façade only dates from 1933, when Mussolini altered the frontage of so many buildings, the auditorium boasts a wonderful tier of baroque boxes on either side of the stage.

Largo Respighi 1 199 107 070 (Info line call centre) www.comunalebologna.it. Guided tours in English and Italian take place 10.00 (Sun) and 11.00 (Mon); admission charge Bus C

Via delle Moline and Bologna's canals

One of Bologna's early disadvantages was that it had no natural water source, so in the 12th century a canal system was put in place that dammed water from the Reno River to divert into the city. This not only provided much-needed drinking water and sanitation, as well as powering the silk and hemp mills that were at the centre of Bologna's trade in the Middle Ages, but it also allowed goods and materials to be imported and exported north to the River Po. By the early 20th century, however, industrialisation and the advent of motor traffic meant that the canals had become redundant, and they were paved over. Some are just visible, though: at the bridges on Via Piella, Via Capo di Lucca and Via Alessandrini you can still see water flowing beneath the streets.

Via San Vitale

This is the place to come if you're in search of antiques, or simply want to escape the lively student atmosphere of Via Zamboni. But it's also worth visiting for the palazzi behind the long portico, some of which are open to the public. Palazzo Orsi at No 28 is known for its baroque statues, the façade of Palazzo Fantuzzi at No 23 is decorated with incongruous elephant motifs, while the Palazzo Scagliarini-Rossi at No 56 was the 19th-century home of Cornelia Rossi, a legendary society hostess in her day.

ⓐ Via San Vitale ⓝ Bus 14, 19, 25, 27, C

CULTURE

Conservatorio di Musica G B Martini and Museo Bibliografico Musicale

When Napoleon briefly conquered Italy at the turn of the 19th century, he deconsecrated many buildings, including this former Augustine convent. Instead, it became Bologna's music conservatory, which can count many great musicians and composers among its alumni, including Verdi, Rossini and Puccini. The highlight of the conservatory is the concert hall, with a huge organ at its heart and the walls decorated with portraits of composers down the centuries. There is also a musical museum on site, containing many priceless works, including autographed scripts and scores, the original score of Rossini's 1816 opera, *The Barber of Seville*, historic instruments, and portraits of composers, including one of Johann Christian Bach by Thomas Gainsborough.

ⓐ Piazza Rossini 2 ⓣ 222 997/221 117 ⓛ 09.00–13.00 Mon–Sat
ⓝ Bus 14, 19, 25, 27, C

ⓞ *A quiet corner of Europe's oldest university*

Museo Ebraico (Jewish Museum)

When Bologna became a Papal State in the 16th century, the Jewish community, who had previously lived and worked alongside the rest of the population, were forced to move to a gated ghetto on the east side of the historic centre. Nevertheless, they continued to make an important contribution to city life, particularly in trade. This relatively new museum, in the heart of the former ghetto, examines the history of Jews in the city through the ages, including the tragedy of World War II. It also hosts regular lectures and workshops on the theme of Jewish identity, and other related topics.

ⓐ Via Valdonica 1/5 ⓣ 291 1280 ⓦ www.museoebraicobo.it
ⓛ 10.00–18.00 Sun–Thur, 10.00–16.00 Fri; admission charge

Palazzo Poggi and the university museums

Bologna's original university was housed in the Archiginnasio, just off Piazza Maggiore, but in 1803, under the instructions of Napoleon, its faculties were all united under one roof in the Palazzo Poggi, previously home to the Poggi family and then a science laboratory. It remains the main building of the university to this day. The grand interior is decorated with numerous murals, including *Ulysses* by Tibaldi, *The Labours of Hercules* by Nicolo dell'Abate and biblical scenes by Propero Fantana, all dating from the early 16th century.

The palazzo is best known today, however, as home to many of the university museums. The **Museo Navale** has an impressive collection of nautical maps and model warships, the **Museo di Architettura Militare** explores the history of military architecture including models of baroque fortifications, and **Museo di Astronomia** contains many instruments used in the 18th and 19th centuries to study the stars, a fresco of the constellations, and exhibits detailing the history of astronomy.

Palazzo Poggi Via Zamboni 31–33 209 9398 www.unibo.it 10.00–16.00 Mon–Fri, 10.30–17.30 Sat–Sun. Closed Aug Bus Linea C to Teatro Comunale

Pinacoteca Nazionale

Almost no Italian city is without its art treasures, and Bologna's Pinacoteca Nazionale (National Gallery) is a must for art-lovers and historians alike. Among the collections are works by Tibaldi, Reni, the Carracci brothers and Guercino, painters from Bologna's most productive period, the early 17th century. The highlight, however, must be Raphael's *Ecstasy of Saint Cecilia* (c. 1515).

 Via delle Belle Arti 56 420 9411/421 1984 www.pinacotecabologna.it 09.00–19.00 Tues–Sun; admission charge Bus 20, 28, 36, 37, 89, 93, 94, 99

RETAIL THERAPY

Given that this is the university quarter, it's not surprising that the area is famous for its bookshops. Obviously most stock will be in Italian, but larger stores such as Feltrinelli will sell foreign-language books.

Itinerari A quiet, well-stocked travel bookstore. Via San Vitale 51 296 0471 Bus 14, 19, 25, 27, C

Libreria Antiquaria Palmaverde This second-hand and antiquarian bookshop is a favourite with writers. Via dei Poeti 4 232 085 Bus 11, 13

Libreria delle Moline Large selection of new and old books. Favoured by students and bookworms. ⓐ Via delle Moline 3 ⓣ 232 053 Ⓝ Bus 20, 28, 36, 37, C

Libreria Feltrinelli This is the main branch of Italy's largest and best bookstore chain. ⓐ Piazza di Porta Ravegnana ⓣ 261 392 Ⓝ Bus 11, 17, 28, A & C

TAKING A BREAK

Del Museo £ ❶ Decorated in retro style, with dark wood floors, comfy sofas and cosy alcoves, this is perfect for a romantic drink. ⓐ Via Zamboni 58 ⓣ 246 620 Ⓛ Early closing Sat. Closed Aug Ⓝ Bus Linea C

Del Teatro £ ❷ An attractive place for a drink, opposite the Teatro Comunale, hence its name. ⓐ Via Zamboni 26 ⓣ 222 623 Ⓝ Bus Linea C

Bravo ££ ❸ A good-value trattoria that is particularly renowned for its Sunday brunch. ⓐ Via Mascarella 1 ⓣ 266 1122 Ⓛ 12.30–15.30 & 19.00–02.00 Mon–Sun. Closed Aug Ⓝ Bus Linea C

Golem Caffè d'Arte ££ ❹ In the heart of the old Jewish quarter, this small atmospheric place is popular with local artists, not least because the proprietors hang their works on the walls. ⓐ Piazza San Martino ⓣ 262 620 Ⓛ Closed Sun eve Ⓝ Bus 11, 13, 14, 19, C

AFTER DARK

Restaurants

La Mariposa £ ❺ One of the most authentic trattorie in the city and a perennial favourite with the locals. Not only is the food fresh and delicious but it's good value too. ⓐ Via Bertiera 12 ⓣ 225 656 ⓛ Closed Sat eve & Sun ⓝ Bus 20, 27, A, C

La Stanze £ ❻ There's a unique atmosphere here as the restaurant is set in the private chapel of the Nuovo Palazzo Bentivoglio built in 1576. You can gaze at the 16th-century frescoes adorning the walls while tucking in to a simple but good plate of pasta. ⓐ Via del Borgo di San Pietro 1 ⓣ 228 767 ⓛ 11.00–01.30 Mon–Fri, 18.00–24.00 Sat. Closed July & Aug ⓝ Bus 20, 28, 36, 37, 89, 93, 94, 99

Osteria dell'Orsa £ ❼ Famous for its *ragù alla Bolognese*, this place is a favourite hangout for students. ⓐ Via Mentana 1 ⓣ 231 576 ⓛ until 01.00 Mon–Sun ⓝ Bus Linea C

Benso ££ ❽ Tucked into a side street in the old Jewish ghetto, this family-owned restaurant serves traditional Bolognese cuisine. They are particularly known for their desserts, such as *gelato ripieno all frutta* (fruit-filled ice cream). There is also a courtyard for dining alfresco. ⓐ Vicolo San Giobbe 3 ⓣ 223 904 ⓛ Closed Sun ⓝ Bus 14, 19, 25, 27

Bars, Clubs & Discos

Kinki ❾ A gay-friendly disco where a lot of tourists go. House and techno music. ⓐ Via Zamboni 1 ⓣ 226 028 ⓛ 23.00–04.00

La Scuderie ⑩ Bar, restaurant, music and dance venue, La Scuderie is always busy. ⓐ Piazza Verdi 2 ⓣ 656 9619 ⓛ 08.00–02.00 Mon–Sun

Music
Two good venues for music in this area are:

Stadio R Dall'Ara A little way outside the city, this is the main venue for rock concerts by both Italian and visiting bands. ⓐ Via A Costa 174 Ⓝ Bus 14, 21

Teatro Comunale The city's traditional classical music venue, in existence since the 18th century. Also the venue for the acclaimed opera season from November through to June. Tickets are available from the box office, but for the opera you'll need to book well in advance. ⓐ Largo Respighi 1 ⓣ 199 107 070 (Info line call centre) Ⓦ www.comunalebologna.it Ⓝ Bus C

Theatre
Among the theatres in this area are:

Arena del Sol ⓐ Via Indipendenza 44 ⓣ 291 0910 Ⓦ www.arenadelsole.it Ⓝ Bus 27 from Piazza XX Settembre

Teatro Dehon ⓐ Via Libia 59 ⓣ 342 934 or 344 772 Ⓦ www.teatrodehon.it Ⓝ Bus 37 from Stazione Ferroviaria, Bus 14, 25 from Via Massarenti, Bus 20 from Via S. Donato

◀ *Teatro Comunale's beautiful interior*

Santo Stefano & around

Traditionally the eastern side of Bologna has always been the
smartest district and it was in this part of the city that all the noble
families made their home in the Middle Ages.

The main streets – Via Santo Stefano, Via Castiglione, Piazza
Santo Stefano and Strada Maggiore – each have a distinct character
and, given the wealth of the area over the centuries, are naturally
lined with grand palazzi and landscaped gardens as well as
important churches. Strada Maggiore was also once part of the
Roman Via Aemilia, the important trade route that linked Piacenza
and the Adriatic coast.

SIGHTS & ATTRACTIONS

Abbazia di San Stefano

Probably one of the most important areas of worship in Bologna
and a spectacular example of Romanesque architecture, there were
originally seven churches here in total, built in the 8th century over
a pagan temple. Today, however, only four churches remain, dating
from the 11th century. The **Chiesa di Crocifisso** (Church of the
Crucifix) is notable for its simplicity – it has only a nave and a crypt,
but it also leads to the **Chiesa di San Sepolcro**, which contains the
tomb of San Petronio, one of the patron saints of Bologna. So
important was the saint to the city that it was deemed entirely
fitting to offer him such an elaborate burial site, reportedly
modelled on the Holy Sepulchre in Jerusalem. The courtyard of this
church is known as Piazza di Pilatus (Courtyard of Pontius Pilate)
because in ancient times the 8th-century basin of its fountain was
thought to be the one used by Pontius Pilate to wash his hands

Santo Stefano & around

VIALE G CARDUCCI

VIALE G ERCOLANI

PIAZZA DI PORTA MAGGIORE

PIAZZA DI PORTA STEFANO

Casa di Giosuè Carducci

PIAZZETTA MORANDI

VIA DELLA

VIA S GIULIANO

SANTO STEFANO

VIA DEL BARACCANO

Chiesa della Madonna del Baraccano

VIALE G GOZZADINI

STRADA MAGGIORE

Palazzo Hercolani

7

Palazzo Davia Bargellini

Basilica di Santa Maria dei Servi

Giardino di Via dei Bersaglieri

3

Palazzo Zani

Palazzo Pini

6

Palazzo Vizzani

8

Palazzo Fantuzzi

5

Chiesa di San Bartolomeo

Casa Isolani

Abbazia di Santo Stefano

Palazzo Bolognini

Chiesa di San Giovanni in Monte

2

15

Eleonora Duse Theatre

4

PIAZZA DI PORTA CASTIGLIONE

Palazzo della Mercanzia

12

11

Aula Magna Room

14

Loggia dei Carrobbio

Casa Pepoli

10

CASTIGLIONE

Palazzo Pepoli Campogrande

9

PIAZZA MINGHETTI

Museo Civico Archeologico

Palazzo dell'Archiginnasio

Basilica di San Petronio

Chiesa di S Maria della Vita

Palazzo del Podestà

Palazzo Comunale

i

Basilica di San Domenico

10

Palazzo Ruini

13

Portico dell'Annunziata

11

Palazzo Bevilacqua Sanuti

1

Chiesa di S Procolo

Chiesa di San Giovanni Battista dei Celestini

Palazzo Salina-Amorini

Basilica di S Paolo

Chiesa di S Maria delle Muratelle

Chiesa di San Salvatore

Palazzo Caprara

- ✝ Cathedral
- *i* Information
- ✈ Airport
- 🚉 Railway Stn
- 🚌 Bus Station
- ✚ Hospital

0   100 metres
0   100 yards

after he condemned Christ to death. The Romanesque cloisters of this church complex feature a series of plaques commemorating citizens of Bologna who have given their lives in times of war.

Outside the church the cobblestones of the triangular Piazza Santo Stefano are one of the most photogenic areas of the city.
ⓐ Via Santo Stefano 24 ⓣ 223 256 ⓞ 09.00–12.00 & 15.30–18.30 daily. Free ⓝ Bus 14, 19, 25, 27

Basilica di Santa Maria dei Servi

The first things to strike you about this Gothic 14th-century church are the frescoes by Vitale da Bologna, considered by many to be the 'father' of Bolognese painting. His work features in abundance in the interior, too, but the most priceless artwork is the *Madonna and Child* by Cimabue. The convent and sacristy also house 17th- and 18th-century paintings by artists from the acclaimed Bologna School.
ⓐ Strada Maggiore 43 ⓣ 226 807 ⓞ 07.00–11.45 & 15.45–19.45 daily ⓝ Bus 14, 19, 25, 27

Chiesa di San Giovanni in Monte

Although the body of this church was built in the 13th century, the façade that greets visitors today is 15th-century, constructed in Venetian style. The interior, however, is pure Gothic, and enhanced by artworks by the likes of Francesco del Cossa, Guercino, and the *Crowning of the Virgin* altarpiece by Lorenzo Costa. Above the wooden door is a terracotta statue of an eagle, the symbol of St John, by Niccolò dell'Arca.
ⓐ Via Monticelli ⓞ 08.00–12.00, 15.00–18.00 Mon–Sun ⓝ Bus 14, 19, 25, 27

◖ *Romanesque architecture of San Stefano*

Conservatorio and Chiesa della Madonna del Baraccano

After walking through an elegant 15th-century portico you reach the Chiesa della Madonna del Baraccano, commissioned by Giovanni Bentivoglio II (see page 71) who added so much to Bologna's landscape. Above the church is the Conservatorio del Baraccano, established in 1531 as a school for poor girls.

ⓐ Piazza del Barracano 2 ☎ 392 680 🕒 10.00–13.00 & 16.00–19.00 Sat–Sun Ⓝ Bus 11, 19

Casa Isolani and Corte Isolani

Via Santo Stefano and the Strada Maggiore are linked by a pretty passageway via a string of courtyards, dating from the 12th to the 16th centuries and today filled with restaurants, boutiques and cafés. At the end of the passageway are two houses, Le Casa Isolani, which belonged to rich merchants during the Middle Ages who made their livings selling Grecian wares. The house on Piazza Santo Stefano features a spiral staircase by Vignola, while the one on Strada Maggiore has an impressive 10-m (30-ft) high portico.

Ⓝ Bus 11, 13, 19, 90, 96

Loggia del Carrobbio

Since being built by Antonio di Vincenzo and Lorenzo da Bagnomarino in 1384, this has been the seat of the Chamber of Commerce, Industry, Agriculture and Crafts for Bologna. Constructed of brick and Istrian stone, the main feature of the façade is its Gothic arches. The stunning columns and balcony are by the father and son team of Giovanni and Pietro di Giacomo.

ⓐ Piazza della Mercanzia, Via Santo Stefano ☎ 609 3111
🕒 09.00–12.00 & 14.00–17.00 Mon–Sun (access to entrance hall only) Ⓝ Bus 11, 13, 14, 19, 20, 25, 27, 29, 30, A, B

Palazzo Bolognini

A short walk up Via Santo Stefano from the loggia brings you to what was the house of another of Bologna's powerful families, the Bologninis, whose chapel is a feature of the San Petronio church (see page 62). Dating from the 16th century, the house has the nickname Palazzo delle Teste (Palace of the Heads), because of the many busts that look down onto the street. They are attributed to the sculptor Alfonso Lombardi (1487–c.1536).

Via Santo Stefano 9/11 Bus 14, 19, 25, 27

Piazza San Domenico

The main feature of this quiet square is the **Basilica di San Domenico**, whose highlight is undoubtedly the *arca* or canopy to the tomb of the saint by 13th-century sculptor Nicola Pisano with contributions from other Bolognese artists. The canopy was designed by an artist entitled Niccolò de Bari but it was so admired that he was forever after referred to as Niccolò dell'Arca. He died before all the statuettes were done, leaving the figures of San Petronius and San Procolus to be completed by his student, Michelangelo. Michelangelo also carved the kneeling angel on the front of the tomb.

In the centre of the square is a column topped with a statue of the Virgin Mary that gives thanks for the end of a plague in 1632.

Bus 11, 13, 14, 19, 25, 27

Strada Maggiore

This has been one of Bologna's most important streets since ancient times, forming part of the Roman Via Aemilia (see page 92): within the shop at No 11 you can see a small piece of the original road that has been excavated and preserved. Today the street is lined with a

series of former noble residences. At No 44 the most striking feature of the **Palazzo Davia Bargellini** façade is its two statues of Atlas on both sides of the entrance, supporting the balcony above. The building is now home to the Galleria Davia Bargellini (🕒 09.00–13.00 Tues–Sun), which displays the art collection of this noble family, This spans the 14th to 18th centuries and includes a *Madonna and Child* by Cristoforo da Bologna and *La Pietà* by Simone dei Crocefissi. In the same building is the Museo Civico d'Arte Industriale with its collection of textiles, glassware and furniture from various eras

Galleria Davia Bargellini & Museo Civico d'Arte Industriale ⓐ Strada Maggiore 44 ❶ 236 708 🕒 09.00–14.00 Tues–Sat, 09.00–13.00 Sun Ⓝ Bus 14, 19, 25, 27

Via Santo Stefano

Via Santo Stefano is most notable for its impressive mansions that were once home to some of the city's wealthiest families. Also here, at No 31, is the Teatro dal Corso, which is most famous for having witnessed the debut of Gioacchino Rossini in 1811 with his opera *L'equivico stravagante*. The Palazzo Finzi-Contini at No 33 was once a hotel, whose past guests have included the novelist Giorgio Bassani and one of Italy's greatest poets, Giacomo Leopardi.

Ⓝ Bus 14, 19, 25, 27

RETAIL THERAPY

Bang Bang 2 You won't find any bargains here, but you will find collections from several designers under one roof, including Moschino, Versace and Sonia Rykiel. ⓐ Piazzia Mercanzia 5 ❶ 263 814 Ⓝ Bus 14, 19, 25, 27

◀ *Piazza San Domenico*

Branchini Calzoleria Another place to splash your cash (this is the smartest area of the city, after all) on exquisitely cut dresses and hand-stitched shoes. ❸ Strada Maggiore 19 ❶ 648 6642 ◍ Bus 14, 19, 25, 27

Mercato Antiquario One of the best antiques markets in the city – come early if you want to secure the best bargains. ❸ Via Santo Stefano ◷ Sat–Sun every 2nd week ◍ Bus 14, 19, 25, 27

TAKING A BREAK

Bricco d'Oro £ ❶ Morning or afternoon, this is a great spot for a cup of hot chocolate topped with peaks of whipped cream. It's a short walk from Piazza Maggiore, and early evening it makes for a good pre-dinner pit stop for an aperitif. ❸ Via Farini 6 ❶ 236 231 ◍ Bus 11, 13, 19, 29, 38, 30, 52, E

Godot Wine Bar £ ❷ This neighbourhood bar has a remarkable wine list with more than 1,000 wines to choose from, so whatever your grape preferences you should find something you like here. The menu is limited but good, offering selections of mortadella and assorted cheeses. ❸ Via Cartoleria 22 ❶ 226 315 ◷ 08.00–02.00 Mon–Sat ◍ Bus 11, 13, 14, 19

Morandi £ ❸ A locals' favourite, reportedly serving the best cappuccino in town – thick, creamy and full of flavour. ❸ Piazzetta Morandi 1 ❶ 342 734 ◍ Bus 11, 19

Sorbetteria Castiglione £ ❹ Some locals will cross the entire city for the ice creams here. Try out more unusual concoctions such as

mascarpone with caramelized pine nuts and white chocolate and hazelnut crunch. Next door is an equally delectable sweet shop – a chocolate version of the Due Torri is a great souvenir to take home.
🄰 Via Castiglione 44 🕐 233 257 🕒 Closed Tues 🄽 Bus 30, 59, E

Dei Commercianti ££ 🄹 More expensive than most cafés, but the cappuccinos are delicious and the surroundings are elegant.
🄰 Strada Maggiore 23/c 🕐 266 539 🕒 until 22.00 Mon–Sat 🄽 Bus 14, 19, 25, 27

AFTER DARK

Restaurants
Bottega Albertini £ 🄺 Formerly the Sale e Pepe restaurant, the Albertini now serves innovative dishes in a romantic setting. Furthermore, the fixed price of around €15 per person for a three-course meal including wine makes this one of the best deals in town. 🄰 Via de' Coltelli 9/2 🕐 228 532 🕒 Closed Sun 🄽 Bus 11, C

Clorafilla £–££ 🄻 A rare thing in Italy, but this is an organic vegetarian restaurant with a menu that goes to great lengths to explain the health benefits of all the ingredients. Even if you're a committed carnivore, it's a great place for delicious salads.
🄰 Strada Maggiore 64 🕐 235 343 🕒 Closed Sun 🄽 Bus 14, 19, 25, 27, C

Antica Osteria Romagnala ££ 🄼 Housed in a 17th-century building, the Romagnala offers a wonderful array of pastas, as well as another local speciality, *capretto* (roast goat). 🄰 Via Rialto 13 🕐 263 699 🕒 19.30–23.00 Tues, 12.30–14.30 & 19.30–23.00 Wed–Sun 🄽 Bus 11, 13, 19 🄸 Reservations recommended for dinner.

Da Ercole ££ ⑨ Typical Bolognese cuisine, with an emphasis on fish dishes and large salads. Popular with older locals. Located on a leafy piazza, there is seating outside in season.
ⓐ Piazza Minghetti 2 ❶ 228 848 ◷ Closed Mon Ⓝ Bus 11, 13, 19, 20, 29, 30, 90, 96

Degli Angeli ££ ⑩ The name means 'tavern of the angels' and the dishes here certainly are close to heavenly. Simple food, lovingly prepared ⓐ Via Farini 31 ❶ 268 032 ◷ Closed Sat lunch and all of Sun Ⓝ Bus 11, 13, 90, 96, A

Le Mura ££ ⑪ Its out-of-the-way location means that this is more of a locals' haunt, but it's worth the effort to come here and sample the delicious menu at good-value prices. ⓐ Vicolo Falcone 13 ❶ 331 772 ◷ Closed Mon Ⓝ Bus 29, 52

Leonida ££ ⑫ A relaxed, welcoming atmosphere greets diners at this friendly restaurant, where the house specialities are asparagus lasagne and tagliatelle with peas. ⓐ Vicolo Alemagna 2 ❶ 239 742 ◷ Closed Sun Ⓝ Bus 14, 19, 25, 27, C

Trebbi ££ ⑬ You don't stay in business for 50 years if the customers don't like what they're served. Trebbi has been pleasing local palates with its traditional cuisine for half a century.
ⓐ Via Solferino 40 ❶ 583 713 ◷ Closed Sat lunch Ⓝ Bus 15, 16, 29, 30, 39, 59, A, E

Dei Poeti £££ ⑭ One of the oldest osterias in Bologna, the setting of Dei Poeti in the 14th-century Palazzo Senatorio is almost as good

◀ *The food sometimes looks too good to eat*

as its food. For a more lively evening, get a table in the large dining room, where there is live music three times a week. ⓐ Via dei Poeti 1 ⓣ 236 166 ⓒ Closed Mon ⓝ Bus 11, 13, 16, 30, 38, A

Drogheria della Rosa £££ ⓯   A cosy restaurant that used to be a food store, hence the name *drogheria* (which means 'grocer's') and the original doors and furnishings. The food is superb, and there's an exceptional wine list. ⓐ Via Cartoleria 10 ⓣ 266 864 ⓝ Bus Linea C

Bars, Clubs & Discos
Kasamatta ⓰   A very trendy three-floor disco-pub. ⓐ Via Sampieri 3 ⓣ 224 256 ⓒ dancing from 01.00

Music & Theatre
Good venues for music and theatre are:

Accademia Filarmonica ⓐ Via Guerrazzi 13 ⓣ 222 997 ⓦ www.accademiafilarmonica.it

Basilica di Santa Maria dei Servi This lovely church (see page 95) stages classical concerts year round, except in July and August. ⓐ Strada Maggiore 43 ⓣ 226 807 ⓝ Bus 14, 19, 25, 27

Teatro Duse ⓐ Via Castellata 7 ⓣ 213 836 or 800 907 080 ⓦ www.teatroduse.it ⓝ Bus 16, 30, 39, 59, A, C, E

▶ *Piazza Municipio, Ferrara*

OUT OF TOWN
trips

Parma

Even if you've never heard of the town of Parma, the chances are you've eaten its produce. Parma ham and Parmesan cheese grace the menu of every Italian restaurant the world over, while the Barilla empire, which is now one of the world's biggest pasta producers, also has its roots in the city.

But it's not all about food. The city is one of the great cultural centres of Italy, abounding in impressive architecture, sculptures and artworks, in particular the work of native Mannerist artist Francesco Mazzola, more affectionately known as Parmigianino after his home town. Parma is also renowned as an operatic centre – this was the birthplace, after all, of one of the greatest conductors of all time, Arturo Toscanini.

But, culture aside, simply strolling the medieval streets and dining al fresco in this heartland of Italian cuisine is reason enough to visit.

GETTING THERE

There is one bus to Parma, which leaves at 09.40 from the main Bologna bus station on Mondays, Wednesdays and Fridays and returns on the same days at 14.30. The journey takes two hours and is operated by Sena buses. ⓐ Piazza XX Settembre 6 (Via San Vitale), Bologna ⓣ 242 150 ⓦ www.sena.it

The Milan–Bologna rail line runs through Parma. Forty-seven trains a day arrive from Bologna, trip time one hour to Parma. ⓐ Piazzale della Chiesa 11 ⓣ 783 960/147 888 088. For train information and schedules call Trenitalia ⓣ 892 021 (toll free in Italy only) ⓦ www.trenitalia.com

Parma's bus and train stations are a fifteen-minute walk from the

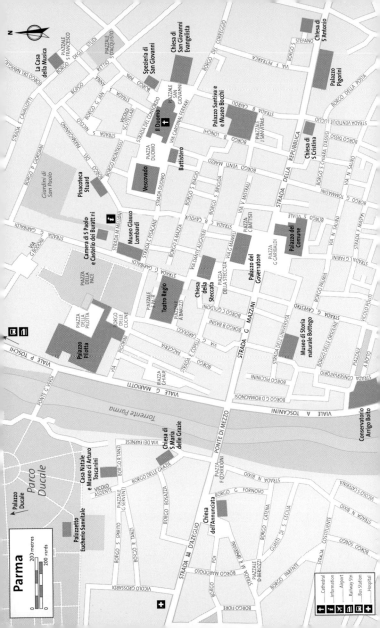

central Piazza Garibaldi, or a short ride on buses Nos 8 or 9. Parma bus station ⓐ Piazza della Chiesa ⓣ 273 251. TEP buses (ⓐ Via Taro 14 ⓣ 0521 2141 ⓦ www.tep.pr.it) service the province of Emilia-Romagna.

If travelling by car, head northwest along A1 from Bologna. While traffic is not too much of an issue in Parma, finding a parking spot can be a real headache. Either park in one of the many paying car parks on the outskirts of the city, or at the bus or train stations, or along the riverfront boulevards behind Palazzo Pilotta.

The main tourist office in Parma is ⓐ Strada Melloni 1/a, off the main Strada Garibaldi ⓣ 0521 218 889 ⓛ 09.00–19.00 Mon–Sat, 09.00–13.00 Sun ⓦ www.turismo.comune.parma.it

SIGHTS & ATTRACTIONS

Chiesa di San Giovanni Evangelista (Church of Saint John the Evangelist)

The most striking feature of this church is the cupola decorated with the 16th-century fresco *Vision of Saint John* by Correggio. Over the door, to the left of the altar, is another painting of Saint John by Correggio. In the chapel on the left of the entrance are frescoes by Il Parmigianino.

ⓐ Piazzale San Giovanni ⓛ 09.00–midday & 15.30–18.00 Mon–Sun

Il Duomo (Cathedral)

This Romanesque cathedral, built in the 11th century, is one of the most dominant features of the Parma landscape, with its elegant tiered loggias looking down over the large square. But to appreciate the true wonders of the building one has to go inside. The main

◖ *The calm cloisters of Chiesa di San Giovanni Evangelista*

feature is the frescoed cupola depicting *The Assumption* (1526) by Antonio da Correggio, but the cathedral abounds with artworks by this great Renaissance painter and by his pupils, including Parmigianino.

Also dominating the square is the octagonal Baptistry, looking slightly Moorish in style with its pink marble, and most noted for its elaborate 12th-century biblical frescoes by Benedetto Antelami.

ⓐ Piazza del Duomo ⓣ 0521 235 886 ⓛ 09.00–12.00 & 15.00–19.00 Mon–Sun ⓝ Bus 11

Baptistry ⓣ 235 886 ⓛ 09.00–12.30 & 15.00–18.30 Mon–Sun ⓝ Bus 11

Palazzo Pilotta

The one-time home of the powerful Farnese family, who virtually ruled Parma for centuries, was rebuilt after being bombed in World War II and is now home to a variety of important museums and institutions. On the second floor is the Galleria Nazionale (National Gallery) with a comprehensive array of paintings from the 13th century right through to the 19th century. Among the artists featured here are Correggio, Canaletto and Leonardo da Vinci, including his masterful *Saint Jerome with the Madonna and Child*.

On the ground and first floors of the palace there is also the Museo Archeologico Nazionale (National Archaeological Museum), which has an impressive array of finds from several great civilisations, including the ancient Greeks, Romans, Egyptians and Etruscans.

Also on the first floor is the renovated 17th-century Teatro Farnese. This spectacular wooden structure shows clear influence from Palladio with its elegant tiered balconies in neoclassical style.

Galleria Nazionale, Palazzo Pilotta ⓐ Piazzale della Pilotta ⓣ 0521 233 309 ⓛ 08.30–13.45 Tues–Sun; admission charge

◀ *The pink marble Baptistery*

Museo Archeologico Nazionale, Palazzo Pilotta ⓐ Piazzale della Pilotta ❶ 0521 233 718 ❷ 09.30–12.30 & 16.00–19.00 Sun only, June, July & Sept, 09.30–12.30 Sun only, Aug; admission charge

Teatro Farnese, Palazzo Pilotta ⓐ Piazzale della Pilotta ❷ 08.30–13.45 Tues–Sun; admission charge

Parco Ducale

Created in the 16th century by the duke of Parma and Piacenza, in the 18th century Philip II of Bourbon commissioned the redesign of these magnificent gardens along rocaille and neoclassical lines. In 2001 the gardens were fully restored to this French style. The gardens are also home to the 16th-century Ducal Palace, the 15th-century Palazzetto Sanvitale and an 18th-century 'little temple', Il Tempietto.

Parco Ducale ⓐ Strada delle Fonderie/Via dei Farnese ❶ 0521 218 889. **Palazzo Ducale** ❷ 09.30–12.00 Mon–Sat; admission charge.

Palazzetto Eucherio Sanvitale ❷ 10.00–13.00, 14.00–16.00 Mon–Sun, Nov–Feb; 10.00–13.00, 14.00–17.00 Mon–Sun, Mar, Apr & Oct; 10.00–13.00, 14.00–18.00 Mon–Sun, May–Sept; admission free.

Gardens ❷ 07.00–20.00 Mon–Sun, Nov–Mar; 06.00–24.00 Mon–Sun Apr–Oct.

Piazza Garibaldi

Indisputably the heart of the city ever since Roman times, this square honours two men important to Parma in differing ways – the great artist Correggio, whose work adorns so many of the churches, and the Italian unifier Garibaldi: they both have statues here.

The two most dominant buildings on the square are the Palazzo del Governatore (Governor's Palace) and the Palazzo del Comune (Town Hall). The former is most notable for its 18th-century

◀ *Piazza Garibaldi*

belltower, which can be climbed for wonderful views of the city, and for its sundials on the front of the building. Opposite the Governor's Palace stands the 17th-century Palazzo del Comune, which is less elaborate in style but is decorated with frescoes on the façade.

Palazzo del Governature belltower ② Piazza Garibaldi ① 0521 212 181 ● 10.00–12.30 & 14.30–16.30 Sat–Sun; admission charge ① Maximum 8 visitors at a time

Palazzo del Comune ② Piazza Garibaldi ● 08.30–13.00 & 14.30–17.30 Mon & Fri

CULTURE

Casa Natale e Museo di Arturo Toscanini (Arturo Toscanini Birthplace and Museum)

The musician and conductor Arturo Toscanini (1867–1957) was born in this house and, although his family moved only a year later, today it is a museum dedicated to his life and work. On display in the individual rooms are items such as his batons, theatre programmes of operas he conducted in Milan, New York and other great cities, as well as personal objects that reflect his family and friendships.

② Via Rodolfo Tanzi 13 ① 0521 285 499 ● 09.00–13.00 & 14.00–18.00 Tues–Sat, 09.00–13.00 Sun; admission charge ② Bus 3, 4, 5, 6, 11 ① No more than 25 people at a time are permitted inside

Teatro Regio

The most important theatre in Parma is its opera house, which opened its doors with a Bellini opera in 1829. Since then it has attracted opera lovers and opera stars from all over the world. The auditorium is

fittingly beautiful with its gilded tiered boxes and ceiling and a 19th-century painting of a classical scene on its safety curtain.
ⓐ Via Garibaldi 16a ⓣ 0521 218 685 ⓛ tours 10.30–noon Mon–Sat; admission charge ⓝ Bus 1, 3, 4, 5, 6, 8, 9, 11

RETAIL THERAPY

Antica Salumeria Farini Close to Piazza Garibaldi, this shop stocks a vast range of cold meats including Parma ham and other local delicacies. You can eat here or buy some of the delicious products, including preserved mushrooms and other vegetables, to take home. ⓐ Via Farini 57 ⓣ 0521 234 417 ⓛ 09.00–13.30, 15.30–19.30 Mon–Wed & Fri–Sat, 09.00–13.30 Thur

Drogheria Gianfranco Pedrelli Another Aladdin's cave of local produce, including balsamic vinegar from Modena and a large range of other goodies. ⓐ Via Spezia 53B

Enoteca Fontana The first port of call for wine lovers, this wine merchant offers bottles from all over the region they often holds tastings too. The staff are extremely knowledgeable. ⓐ Via Farina 24a ⓣ 0521 286 037 ⓝ Bus 1, 3, 4, 5, 6, 9, 11

Salumeria Garibaldi You can find wedges of Parmesan cheese for sale on just about every street corner in town, but, if you want to purchase your cheese in a special setting, this is the place to go. Along with samples, the friendly staff offer advice on which cheese to get. ⓐ Via Garibaldi 42 ⓣ 0521 235 606 ⓝ Bus 1, 3, 4, 5, 6, 9, 11

AFTER DARK

Restaurants

Trattoria Corrieri £–££ Regional cuisine at reasonable prices. Tortellini with cream and ravioli stuffed with braised beef are among the dishes served by the attentive staff in this popular spot. ⓐ Via Conservatorio 1 ⓣ 0521 234 426 ⓛ Closed Sun ⓘ Long queues can form, particularly at the weekends, so it is advisable to book.

Gallo d'Oro ££ Do not be put off by the slightly dated décor – the food is fresh and delicious and locals have been flocking here for years. Try the *salumi misti* made with locally cured hams, and the roasted lamb stuffed with bread, cheese and eggs. ⓐ Borgo della Salina 3 ⓣ 0521 208 846 ⓛ 12.00–15.00 & 19.00–02.00 Mon–Sat ⓝ Bus 1, 3, 4, 5, 6, 9, 11

Parizzi ££ Housed in a gorgeous building that dates from the mid-16th century, this excellent trattoria has been run by the same family since 1958. Under the skylit patio you can enjoy dishes such as *culatelo* (cured ham made from the haunches of wild boar) or a Parmesan soufflé with white truffles or roasted guinea fowl with Fonseca wine. ⓐ Strada della Repubblica 71 ⓣ 0521 285 952 ⓝ Bus 1, 3, 4, 5, 6, 8, 9, 11 ⓘ Reservations required

Nightclubs, cinema & theatre

For some lively after-dinner nightlife, try **Dadaumpa** ⓐ Via Emilio Lepido 48 ⓣ 0521 483 802 ⓦ www.dadaumpa.com, or **Hippopotamus**, just along the road ⓐ Via Emilio Lepido 28. The **Roxy Bar** has live music and internet stations ⓐ Via Emilia Est 142 ⓣ 487 535

ⓞ *Piazza Garibaldi*

Parma has an excellent range of cinemas including **Capitol multiscreen** San Pancrazio, Cinema D'Azeglio, Via D'Azeglio 33 281 138, which shows international films, and – for serious cinephiles – **Cinema Edison** Largo VIII Marzo 33 967 088. There are also four theatres, including the historic **Teatro Regio** Via Garibaldi 16a 0521 039 393 www.teatroregioparma.org, which stages opera and ballet and is home to the annual Verdi Festival.

ACCOMMODATION

Much like Bologna, Parma doesn't really cater to budget travellers, although there are cheaper accommodation options near the railway and bus stations.

Hotels

Leon d'Oro £ This is an option only if you're really on a shoestring budget. All the bathroom facilities are communal, serving the 16 rooms, and there are six flights of stairs with no lift. It's also on a noisy street near the station. Viale Fratti 4 0521 773 182

Albergo Brenta ££ A pleasant, good-value place to stay in the centre – quite a rarity. Family run, and clean, but no mod cons, although all rooms are en suite. Via GB Borghesi, 12 0521 208 093 www.hotelbrenta.it Bus 1, 3, 4, 5, 6, 9, 11

Park Hotel Stendhal ££–£££ Located in the historic centre, this comfortable and popular refurbished hotel overlooks the green space of the Piazzale della Pace Piazzetta Bodoni 3 0521 208 057

Grand Hotel Baglione £££ A sumptuously furnished hotel in the historic centre overlooking the beautiful Parco Ducale (Ducal Park). There is an excellent restaurant serving modern international and traditional Italian cuisine. ⓐ Via Piacenza 12c ⓣ 0521 292 929 ⓦ www.baglionihotels.com

Hostel
Ostello per la Gioventù Cittadella £ Located in Parma's historical centre in the Cittadella Park, this is basic hostel accommodation with dormitory rooms. There's also an adjacent campsite. Breakfast not included. ⓐ Parco Cittadella 5 ⓣ 0521 941 434 ⓒ Open 07.00–09.30 & 17.00–23.30 ⓘ No credit cards

PARMA CUISINE

The reason that the specialities of the Parma region have become so famous and popular is due to the centuries-old techniques still employed in their production. The hard Parmesan cheese (*parmigiano*) is made with semi-skimmed milk, whey, rennet and salt, then shaped into huge rounds, which can weigh more than 30 kg (66 lb). Its hard texture then lends itself to be sliced, shaved or grated over pasta dishes, although it is also delicious on its own, particularly if accompanied by a glass of local red wine. There are different grades of cheese, depending on how long it has been matured, but the best is Parmigiano Reggiano. The whey that is separated from the curds is then used to feed the pigs. These in turn give the town its other great product: cured Parma ham (*prosciutto*).

Ravenna

Ravenna's very existence is due to its proximity to Classe, an important port during the Roman period that at one time served as the capital of the western Roman Empire because of its defensible position. By 476, however, the western Empire had fallen and Ravenna came under the rule of the Christian Ostrogoths. Two hundred years later the Byzantines took control, and it was these two periods that produced the outpourings of artistic creativity that have made Ravenna such a popular destination for visitors to this day. Both the Goths and the Byzantines, wanting to appear both powerful and influential, decorated lavishly. The remnants of their stunning mosaics, particularly in San Vitale, still excite admiration. They have also earned Ravenna a UNESCO World Heritage Site status.

Ravenna is a small town. Most of the sights, shops, restaurants and accommodation are within easy walking distance of each other. Its relaxed atmosphere lends itself to quiet strolls and café lunches, although it does come alive during the annual Ravenna Music Festival each June and July. Opera greats such as Luciano Pavarotti have performed here in the past. ☎ 0544 249 211 for ticket information. The Dante Festival, during which readings of the *Divine Comedy (Divina Commedia)* take place, is sponsored by the church of San Francesco and is held during the second week of September.

GETTING THERE

Ravenna is 80 km (50 miles) from Bologna. There is a frequent rail service from Bologna, and the one-hour journey time makes it an easy day trip from the region's main city. Ravenna's train station is a ten-minute walk from the city centre. There is also a frequent service

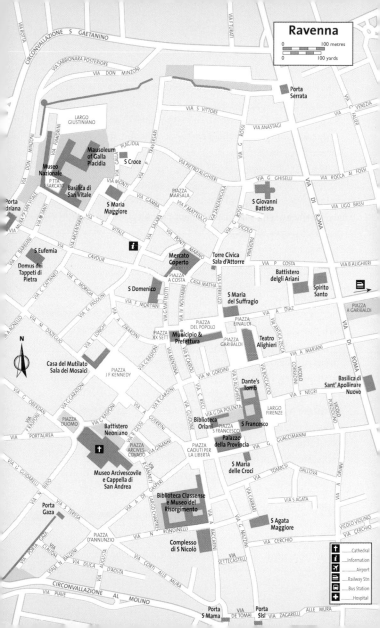

from Ferrara, which connects through Venice. ⓐ Stazione Central, Piazza Farini ❶ 0544 892 021. For train information and schedules call Trenitalia ❶ 892 021 (toll free in Italy only) ⓦ www.trenitalia.com

By car from Bologna, head east along the A14; if coming from Ferrara, take the SS16.

The English-speaking staff at the tourist office are friendly and knowledgeable. Stop in here for maps, information about bicycle rentals (a good way to get around), and a combination ticket to the city's attractions. ⓐ Via Salara 8 ❶ 0544 357 55/354 04 ⓦ www.turismo.ravenna.it

SIGHTS & ATTRACTIONS

The Baptistries

There are two octagonal baptistries in Ravenna that are noted for their mosaics, which depict the Baptism of Christ, surrounded by his 12 Apostles. The **Battistero Neoniano** is considered to be the oldest surviving religious building in Ravenna (5th century), although the **Battistero degli Ariani** is only about half a century younger. Both are now UNESCO World Heritage Sites.

Battistero Neoniano ⓐ Piazza del Duomo ❶ 0544 219 938
🕐 09.00–19.00 Apr–Sept; 09.00–17.30 Mar & Oct; 09.30–16.30 Nov–Feb; admission charge

Battistero degli Ariani ⓐ Via degli Ariani ❶ 0544 434 424
🕐 09.00–19.00 Apr–Sept; 09.00–13.30 Oct–Mar; admission charge

Basilica di Sant'Apollinare Nuovo

This 6th-century church has interior walls decorated with some of the finest mosaics in Ravenna, depicting events from the life of Christ, from birth to Resurrection, as well as images of the prophets and the Apostles. Outside, adjacent to the porticoed façade, there is a 10th-century stone belltower.

ⓐ Via di Roma ⓣ 0544 439 081 ⓛ 09.00–19.00 Apr–Sept; 09.00–17.30 Mar & Oct; 09.30–16.30 Nov–Feb; admission charge

Basilica San Vitale

The focal point of any visit to Ravenna is the Church of San Vitale. Stepping into the gloomy exterior from the bright sunlight outside does not immediately do its treasures justice, but once your eyes have adjusted you are met with a quite extraordinary sight – dazzling gold and glass mosaics dating from the 5th century AD. Even more fascinating is that these mosaics survive not only as some of the last great works of art of the ancient world, but also as one of Christianity's first. Building of the church began in 525 during the reign of Theodoric the Ostrogoth – by the time it was finished, 23 years later, Ravenna was in the hands of the Byzantine emperor Justinian. Indeed, it is thought that San Vitale provided the inspiration for the masterful Hagia Sofia in Istanbul.

Based on two concentric octagons, the central dome is supported by eight columns with recesses emanating from each side. In one of these recesses is the breathtaking semicircular apse covered with an intricate gold mosaic, depicting Christ with San Vitale. The archbishop of Ravenna and Emperor Justinian are also heavily featured, as is Theodora, an Evita-esque figure of the Byzantine Empire who progressed from dancing girl to empress through feminine guile. Daylight streaming in from the arched windows only adds to the glow of the mosaics here.

The choir area, too, has some spectacular mosaic work, this time deviating away from the usual gold colour scheme to bring in the greens and blues of nature and the multicoloured plumage of birds.

There are also biblical themes from the Old and New Testaments, with mosaics depicting Abraham and Christ's Apostles, among other things. In front of the choir is a mosaic maze on the floor, which was a fairly standard addition in Roman times.

Aside from the mosaics – as if there needed to be any more attractions – other features of the church include walls covered in a thin sheet of precious marbles from all over the Mediterranean, an altar dating from the 6th century, ancient reliefs of the *Throne of Neptune* and the *Sacrifice of Isaac* near the choir, and the sarcophagus of Quintus Bonus, complete with reliefs of the Magi and of Daniel in the lions' den.

ⓐ San Vitale 17 ✆ 0544 219 938 🕐 09.00–19.00 Mon–Sun, Apr–Sept; 09.00–17.30 Mon–Sun, Mar–Oct; 09.00–16.30 Mon–Sun, Nov–Feb; admission charge Ⓝ Bus 10, 11

Mausoleo di Galla Placidia (Galla Placidia's Mausoleum)

Built in a cross shape between AD 425 and 433, the mausoleum houses the oldest of Ravenna's mosaics; these are exceptionally vivid, utlilising peacock blue, moss green, gold, deep purple and burnt orange. It's certainly elaborate for a burial place of one of the most controversial women in Roman history. Galla Placidia was the sister of Honorious, one of Rome's last emperors. When the Goths sacked Rome, Galla was taken hostage – and shocked everyone by marrying one of her kidnappers, Ataulf. She battled beside him as they headed south, reigning jointly with him over the Gothic kingdom. When her husband was killed she returned to the Romans, married a Roman general, Constantius, and bore him a son, who became the emperor Valentinian III at the age of six, as his regent Galla took control of the

◀ *A side altar in Basilica San Vitale*

western Roman Empire. She eventually died in Rome in AD 450 but, having given much funding to Ravenna's churches during her lifetime, she is honoured here with this impressive tomb.

🅐 Via San Vitale 🕿 0544 215 193 🕒 09.00–19.00 Mon–Sun, Apr–Sept; 09.00–17.30 Mon–Sun, Mar–Oct; 09.00–16.30 Mon–Sun, Nov–Feb; admission charge 🅝 Bus 10, 11

Piazza del Popolo

During the Byzantine period, Venice became a great world power and briefly ruled a large part of Italy, including Ravenna, during which time the Venetians built this square. They governed from the mid-15th-century Palazzetta Veneziana and oversaw the

● *Visit the tomb of one of Italy's most revered poets, Dante*

construction of the two towers honouring the town's patron saints, San Vitale and Sant'Apollinare.

North of Piazza del Popolo on Via Ponte Marino is Ravenna's medieval leaning tower, the 12th-century Torre Pubblica, which is now supported by steel struts.

Tomba di Dante (Dante's Tomb)

Italy's finest poet, Dante Alighieri was exiled from his native Florence as the political rivalries between the Vatican and the Holy Roman Empire were being waged, and he eventually died in Ravenna in September 1321, not long after he completed the third part of his *Divine Comedy* trilogy: *Paradiso* (Paradise). Given his revered status in Italy, his tomb is surprisingly simple but, by way of posthumous apology, the lamp is kept alight by oil donated from Florence. Near the tomb is the 5th-century church of San Francesco, where Dante's funeral took place, and on the first floor is the Museo Dantesco, which has a collection of paintings, sculptures and books connected to the poet.

Museo Dantesco ⓐ Via Dante Alighieri ❶ 0544 302 52 ⓛ 09.00–noon, 15.30–18.00 Tues–Sun (morning only Oct–Mar); admission charge Ⓝ Bus 3, 10, 11

CULTURE

Museo Arcivescovile e Cappella di San Andrea (Archepiscopal Museum and Chapel of San Andrea

Ravenna's Archbishop's Palace was built in the 6th century under the guidance of Archbishop Maximian, and the main attraction here now is his ivory throne. In the chapel of San Andrea are yet more mosaics, notable not just for their design and colours, but for the rather shocking image of Christ as a warrior. This step away from his

traditionally peaceful image possibly reflects the troubled times that existed during the construction of the work.

ⓐ Piazza Arcivescovile, in the Archbishop's Palace ⓣ 0544 391 96
ⓛ 09.00–19.00 Mon–Sun, Apr–Sept; 09.00–17.30 Mon–Sun, Mar–Oct; 09.00–16.30 Mon–Sun, Nov–Feb; admission charge ⓝ Bus 1, 11

Museo Nazionale (National Museum)

The early Christian and Byzantine eras were so important to Ravenna that this museum is certainly not to be missed if you want to understand the period. Among the archaeological objects housed here dating from that time are paintings, tapestries, burial items, weaponry and much more.

ⓐ Via Fiandrini, adjacent to Via San Vitale ⓣ 0544 312 41
ⓛ 08.30–19.30 Tues–Sun; admission charge ⓝ Bus 10, 11

RETAIL THERAPY

Studio Akomena Since Ravenna is best known for its mosaics, buying a replica makes for the ideal souvenir. Here you'll find all manner of religious copies in the traditional golden hues. ⓐ Via Ponte Delle Vecchia ⓣ 0544 554 700 ⓝ Bus 3, 10, 11

AFTER DARK

Ristorante La Gardela ££–£££ A lovely traditional restaurant near most of Ravenna's main sights. The speciality here is *tortelloni della casa* – pasta served with cream, spinach, tomatoes and herbs. Or try the ravioli stuffed with truffles, or tagliatelle with porcini mushrooms. There's also a good wine list. ⓐ Via Monte Marino 3 ⓣ 0544 217 147 ⓛ 12.00–14.30 & 19.00–22.00 Fri–Wed

ACCOMMODATION

Accommodation in Ravenna, as in the rest of the region, is not cheap on the whole; however, there is one hostel and a few bed and breakfasts that offer simple but clean options. The staff at the tourist office can recommend accommodation, but expect to pay top price in the high season.

Ostello Dante Alighieri £ The area's only hostel is situated east of the train station and fills up fast in summer, so book ahead if you're on a tight budget. Guests are not allowed to be in the hostel between 10.00 and 17.00, and there's an evening curfew of 23.30. ⓐ Via Nicolodi 12 ⓣ 0544 421 164 ⓔ hostelravenna@hotmail.com ⓝ Bus 1, 70 from outside the train station

Hotel Argentario ££ Conveniently situated near the historic centre and the railway station, this is a comfortable and clean hotel. Rooms have en-suites, mini-bars and air conditioning, and buffet breakfast is included. ⓐ Via di Roma 45 ⓦ www.hotelargentarioravenna.it

Hotel Centrale Byron ££ Nicely decorated in art deco style and benefiting from a very central location, just a few steps from Piazza del Popolo. ⓐ Via IV Novembre 14 ⓣ 0544 212 225 ⓕ 341 14 ⓦ www.hotelbyron.com ⓝ Bus 10, 11

Jolly Hotel Mameli ££ Part of the 45-strong Jolly Hotel chain, this is a modern, comfortable and conveniently situated hotel with friendly staff, bright and airy public areas, lifts and private parking. There is a bar and restaurant; an excellent buffet breakfast is included in the price. ⓐ Piazza Mameli 1 ⓣ 0544 357 62 ⓦ www.jollyhotels.it

Ferrara

The strongest influence on the landscape of Ferrara was the powerful d'Este family, who ruled the town from the 13th century to the 16th century, during the height of the Renaissance. The city walls, which they constructed, still stand, and the works of the 15th-century artists of the Ferrara School, including Cosme Tura, Ercole de'Roberti, Lorenzo Costa and Francesco del Cossa, are among the main attractions for visitors today. Poets were also patronised by the d'Este family and produced three of the Italian Renaissance's greatest works: Boiardo's *Orlando Innamorato* in 1483, Ariosto's better-known continuation of the same story *Orlando Furioso* in 1532, and Tasso's *Gerusalemme Liberata* in 1581. Today the city is one of the best preserved in terms of Renaissance architecture and is ideal for strolling around.

Ferrara's Palio di San Giorgio – dating from the 13th century and the oldest in the world – is a local highlight. It is held in the Piazza Ariostea the last Sunday of May (see page 14; ⓦ www.paliodiferrara.it).

Some excellent jazz and classical concerts are the main events of the Estate a Ferrara, an outdoor festival that begins in early July and runs until late August. Also in July is the Ferrara Buskers' Festival, in which street musicians from all over the world descend on the town to play and sing for the locals.

GETTING THERE

Ferrara is around 50 km (30 miles) northeast of Bologna. If travelling from Bologna by car, take the A13 north. Ferrara is situated on the main railway line from Bologna to Padua and Venice, and there are

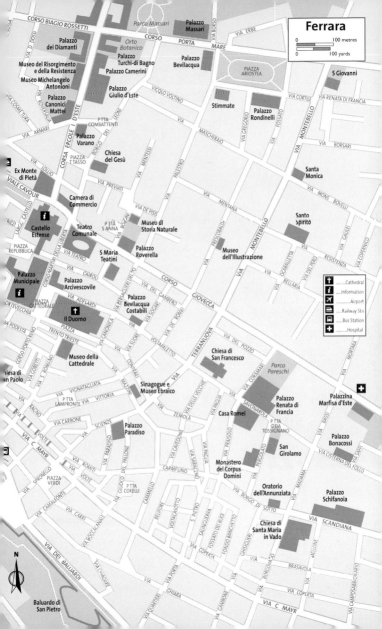

frequent trains. The rail journey time from Bologna to Ferrara is only 30 minutes, making it an easy day trip from the city. Ferrara's train station is west of the city walls, a fifteen-minute walk along Viale Cavour to the centre of town, or a ride on bus Nos 1, 2, 9, 3C. For information and train schedules call Trenitalia ① 0532 892 021 (toll free in Italy only) Ⓦ www.trenitalia.com

The main tourist office is at Castollo Estense. From here you can pick up free maps and get advice on accommodation. ⓐ Piazza del Costello Estense ① 0532 299 303 Ⓦ www.ferrarainfo.com Ⓜ Bus 1, 2, 4, 9

SIGHTS & ATTRACTIONS

Castello Estense

The d'Este family may have been powerful, but they certainly weren't popular among Ferrara's over-taxed citizens, so the wide moat surrounding their dynastic home was probably a necessity rather than a design feature.

The castle was commissioned by Nicolò II, who began construction on 29 September 1385 and ended up with a striking, fortress-style medieval edifice dominating the town with its imposing towers. His son, Nicolò III, was the man largely responsible for its interior style. A tyrant in his personal life (he ordered the assassination of his first wife when he discovered she was having an affair), he was nevertheless an avid patron of the arts, and his taste is reflected in the décor.

Much of the castle is now occupied by office space, but there are a few rooms that have been preserved to illustrate the d'Estes'

◀ Castello Estense

presence here, including the Salone dei Giochi (Games Room), decorated with frescoes by Sebastiano Filippi, depicting sports popular at the time such as discus-throwing, chariot-racing and wrestling.

ⓐ Largo Castello ❶ 0532 299 233 ⓛ 09.30–17.30 Tues–Sun
Ⓝ Bus 1, 2, 4, 9

City walls

Ferrara's impressive medieval walls surround the city for 9 km (5.5 miles), punctuated at certain points by bastions, gateways and towers. They were built at the instigation of Alfonso I in order to protect the d'Este dynasty. When the family was banished to Modena by the Pope in 1598, however, it was exactly these same walls through which they had to depart their city. Today the walls offer great views of both the city and the surrounding landscape, and make an ideal location for cycling or for picnicking.

● *Il Duomo and Museo Cattedrale*

Il Duomo

Opposite the Palazzo Municipale is the magnificent 12th-century cathedral that is designed in a striking combination of Gothic and Romanesque styles. Its façade dominates the square, with its triple roofs and tiered loggias and bas-reliefs illustrating the Last Judgement. The statue in the alcove over the main door is a sculpture of Saint George by Nicholaus. The unfinished campanile (belltower) was designed by Leon Battista Alberti. In contrast to the façade, the interior is more baroque in style. There's also a museum attached to the cathedral that contains artworks dating from the 15th century and various marble sculptures.

ⓐ Piazza Cattedrale ⓘ 0532 207 449 ⓛ 09.00–13.00 & 15.00–18.00 Tues–Sun; admission free but donations appreciated ⓝ Bus 2, 3C

Palazzo dei Diamanti

For art lovers, the best place to see works of artists of the Ferrara School is in the Pinocoteca Nazionale (National Gallery) in the Palazzo dei Diamanti (Diamond Palace), so named because its exterior stone decorations are carved in the shape of diamond points. Inside are works by Cosimo Tura, Francesco Cossa and Lorenzo Costa, among others. There's also a gallery of modern art here, with works by artists such as Gauguin and Klimt.

ⓐ Corso Ercole d'Este 21 ⓘ 0544 205 844 ⓛ 09.00–14.00 Tues–Sat, 09.00–13.00 Sun; admission charge

Palazzo Municipale

South of the Castello Estense is the Palazzo Municipale (Town Hall), which built in 1243, soon after Azzo d'Este seized control of the city. Given its age and importance, restoration work is ongoing, so il

is not always open to the public. Its main attraction is in any case its façade, particularly the bronze statues of Nicolò III on horseback and his son and heir, Borso, sitting on his throne.

Bus 2, 3C

Palazzo Schifanoia

The Schifanoia Palace was built in 1385 by Albert V d'Este and was enlarged by Borso d'Este from 1450 to 1471. The family used this rather than the Castello Estense as their summer residence. The main interest for visitors today is the Salone dei Mesi (Room of the Months), where masterful murals illustrate the twelve months of the year. Each month is subdivided into three horizontal bands – the lower band shows scenes from everyday life in the town at that time of year, the middle shows the relative sign of the zodiac, and the upper depicts the classical god assigned to the month. The works are generally attributed to Cosme Tura, the official court painter who founded the Ferrarese School of art.

Also in the palazzo is the Civic Museum of Ancient Art, which displays, among other things, ancient coins, bronzes and Renaissance plates and pottery.

Via Scandiana 23 0544 641 78 09.30–18.00 Tues–Sun Bus 1, 9

RETAIL THERAPY

Ceramica Artista Ferrarese A wonderful shop selling locally crafted and brightly decorated ceramics, making ideal gifts or souvenirs.
Via Baludardi 125 0544 660 93

Every Tues–Sun from 09.00–13.00 the open-air antiques and crafts market at **Piazza Municipale** features antiques, bric-a-brac and a

range of second-hand goods. The atmosphere is boisterous and bustling, and you never know what treasures you might find.
🚍 Bus 2, 3C

AFTER DARK

Max £–££ There's a student atmosphere here; all come to enjoy the relaxed ambience and the extensive wine list. 🅰 Piazza delle Repubblica 16 ☎ 0544 209 309 🚍 Bus 1, 9

La Provvidenza £££ A wonderfully romantic dinner option, particularly in warm weather when you can dine outside as the sun goes down. Portions of dishes such as fettucine with smoked salmon are very large, so if you like dessert, it might be best to forgo a starter. 🅰 Corso Ercole I d'Este 92 ☎ 0544 205 187 🕐 12.00–15.30 & 19.30–22.30 Tues–Sun 🚍 Bus 3, 9 ❶ Reservations recommended

ACCOMMODATION

There are a number of affordable hotels in Ferrara, most of them near the city centre.

Hotels
Hotel Europa £ A good-value city-centre option with friendly staff and en-suite rooms. An added advantage is that it offers parking facilities for a minimal extra charge. 🅰 Corso della Giovecca 49 ☎ 0544 205 456 🌐 www.hoteleuropaferrara.com 🚍 Bus 1, 2, 3, 9

Locanda Borgonuovo £–££ This elegant bed and breakfast is set in a 17th-century former monastery near Castello Estense. The large

rooms are elegantly decorated with antiques and are all en suite. Breakfast is included and is served in the garden in warm weather. ⓐ Via Cairoli 29 ⓣ 0544 211 100 ⓦ www.borgonuovo.com ⓝ Bus 1, 2, 4, 9 ⓘ Reservations strongly recommended

Hotel Annunziata ££ A lovely hotel that mixes sharp modern décor with 17th-century beams, located directly opposite the Castello Estense (there are also suites in a separate 13th-century building in the grounds of the hotel). Buffet breakfast is included in the price. ⓐ Piazza Repubblica 5 ⓣ 0544 201 111 ⓦ www.annunziata.it

Hostels

Ostello Ferrara Northwest of the city centre, the rooms are unusually large here and very clean, but all bathroom facilities are shared. Reception is closed 10.00–15.30, so you'll need to be out of the hostel during those hours, and the evening curfew is 23.30. ⓐ Via Corso Biagio Rossetti 24 ⓣ 0544 204 227 ⓔ hostelferrara@hotmail.com ⓝ Bus 3

Estense Another simple but clean hostel on the northeast edge of town, open all year. ⓐ Via Gramicia 76 ⓣ 0544 752 396 ⓔ campeggio.estence@libero.it ⓝ Bus No 1 from the train station to Piazzale San Giovanni by the walls; from there it is a 10-minute walk north.

● *Take shelter from the sun in the cloisters of San Domenico*

Directory

GETTING THERE

By air

If Bologna is the only place you will be visiting on your trip, travelling there by air is usually the most cost-effective way to go, particularly as it is now served from the UK by low-cost airlines. Fares will depend on what season you choose to travel, the highest being at Easter, during the Festa di San Luca in May (see page 66), any time between June to mid-August and Christmas to New Year. Prices are considerably lower during the seasons of September to October and November to March, when the city is also considerably less crowded. Weekend trips are usually around 10 per cent more expensive than weekday air fares.

The low-cost airline Ryanair offers fares that can range from around £20 (if booked early enough) to £100 from London Stansted to Forlí airport, which is about 80 km (50 miles) from Bologna. There's a one-hour train ride to the city or a 1½ hour bus trip. There are also frequent flights on British Airways and Alitalia to Bologna from London Gatwick. Bologna is also connected by direct flights to many European cities including Amsterdam, Barcelona, Brussels, Copenhagen, Frankfurt, Lyon, Lisbon, Madrid, Nice, Paris, Vienna and Zurich. Aer Lingus operates flights from Dublin to Bologna.

The top four online booking sites are:

Expedia Ⓦ www.expedia.co.uk
Orbitz Ⓦ www.orbitz.com
Priceline Ⓦ www.priceline.com
Travelocity Ⓦ www.travelocity.com

Ⓓ *Neptune fountain, Piazza Maggiore – the picture every visitor takes*

Some others that offer good deals and links to other discount websites are:

European Travel Network Ⓦ www.etn.nl/discount.htm, or try Ⓦ www.deckchair.com; Ⓦ www.hotwire.com; Ⓦ www.skyscanner.net and Ⓦ www.travelsupermarket.com

Airlines

Aer Lingus, in UK Ⓣ 0870 876 5000. In Republic of Ireland Ⓣ 0818 365 0000 Ⓦ www.aerlingus.ie

Alitalia, in UK Ⓣ 0870 544 8259. In Republic of Ireland Ⓣ 00353 1 677 5171, 00353 1 677 5171 Ⓦ www.alitalia.co.uk

British Airways in UK Ⓣ 0870 850 9850. In Republic of Ireland Ⓣ 1 800 616 747 Ⓦ www.britishairways.com

Ryanair, in UK Ⓣ 0871 246 0000. In Republic of Ireland Ⓣ 0818 303 030 Ⓦ www.ryanair.com

Many people are aware that air travel emits CO_2, which contributes to climate change. You may be interested in the possibility of lessening the environmental impact of your flight through the charity Climate Care, which offsets your CO_2 by funding environmental projects around the world. Visit Ⓦ www.climatecare.org

By rail

The easiest way to take the train to Bologna from the UK is by Eurostar from London Waterloo to Paris, then take a train from Paris to Milan, and again from Milan to Bologna. The journey time is approximately 18–20 hours.

Eurail Ⓦ www.eurail.com

Eurostar Ⓣ 0870 518 6186 Ⓦ www.eurostar.co.uk

InterRail ☎ 0870 084 1411 Ⓦ www.interrail.com
Rail Europe ☎ 08708 30 20 08 Ⓦ www.raileurope.co.uk

The Europe-wide InterRail and Eurail passes give unlimited travel on the Italian national train network.

By bus

If you're really on a shoestring budget, National Express does offer overland European services, but it's not recommended unless you're touring Europe as a whole. The journey time between London and Bologna is around 36 long, boring hours.
National Express Eurolines ☎ UK 0870 058 08080 ☎ Ireland 01 836 6111 Ⓦ www.eurolines.co.uk

By car

The main motorway (*autostrada*) into Bologna is the A1, which comes south from eastern France and through Milan and Parma.

You must be over 18 years of age to drive a car in Italy and have a valid driving licence. Driving is on the right-hand side of the road.

ENTRY FORMALITIES

British, Irish and other European Union (EU) citizens can enter Italy and stay as long as they want by producing a valid passport with photo identification. Citizens of the United States, Canada, Australia and New Zealand need only a valid passport, also with photo identification, but are limited to stays of three months. All other nationals should consult the relevant embassies about visa or passport requirements.

There are no embassies in Bologna itself – the nearest main embassies are in Rome. Bologna does, however, have consulates for the following countries:

Austria ⓐ Via Ugo Bassi 13 ⓣ 268 711
Belgium ⓐ Viale Repubblica 13 ⓣ 505 101
France ⓐ Via Guerazzi 1 ⓣ 230 505
Germany ⓐ Piazza Calderini 2 ⓣ 273 790
Holland ⓐ Via Clavature 22 ⓣ 234 115
South Africa ⓐ Via Saragozza 12 ⓣ 331 306

Embassies in Rome
Australia ⓐ Corso Trieste 25 ⓣ 06 852 721, toll free 800 877 790
Canada ⓐ Via Zara 30 ⓣ 06 445 981
Ireland ⓐ Piazza Campitelli 3 ⓣ 06 697 9121
New Zealand ⓐ Via Zara 28 ⓣ 06 441 7171
United Kingdom ⓐ Via XX Settembre 80a ⓣ 06 422 00001
United States ⓐ Via Veneto 119a ⓣ 06 46 741

In terms of carriage of goods, there are almost no restrictions on what legal goods can be imported or exported to and from other EU countries, as long as you can prove that they are for your own use and not for resale. Anything more than 3,000 cigarettes or 90 litres of wine, for instance, would be considered suspicious and questions will be asked. To import tobacco or alcohol you must be over the age of 17.

For visitors from outside the EU, the restrictions on importing are as follows:
400 cigarettes; or 100 cigarillos; or 50 cigars; or 250 g of tobacco
60 cc of perfume

○ *Bologna, city of arcades*

2 litres of still table wine

250 cc of eau de toilette

1 litre of spirits or strong liqueurs over 22 per cent volume; or 2 litres of fortified wine, sparkling wine or other liqueurs

£145 worth of all other goods including gifts and souvenirs.

MONEY

Italy's currency is the euro (€), and notes are issued in denominations of 5, 10, 20, 50, 100, 200 and 500 euros. Coins are issued in denominations of 1, 2, 5, 10, 20 and 50 cents and 1 and 2 euros.

You can order euro notes ahead of your trip from Thomas Cook, American Express and other exchange services, but there are also ATMs at the airport and throughout the city. Banks are open 08.30–13.30 and 14.30–15.30 on weekdays, and closed Sat & Sun. The easiest way to avoid dealing with the exchange bureaux is by using your credit or debit card in ATMs (bancomat/cash machines). Check with your bank to make sure that your personal identification number (PIN) gives you access to ATM machines abroad. ATMs are available at most banks and accept Visa, Cirrus, Eurocheque and other international cards. Bologna's main bank branches are along Via dell'Indipendenza, Via Rizzoli and Via Ugo Bassi. Most of the major credit cards are accepted in all but the smallest of restaurants and shops.

It's always good to have some travellers' cheques on hand when you travel. Try to get them in different denominations, and keep the purchase agreement and a record of the cheques' serial numbers in a different place from the actual cheques. The most widely accepted travellers' cheques are Thomas Cook (Ⓦ www.thomascook.com) and American Express (Ⓦ www.americanexpress.com). If the cheques are lost or stolen be sure to report it immediately to the issuing company. In most cases the cheques will be replaced within 24 hours.

On euro travellers' cheques you should not have to pay any commission when exchanging them for euros. For other currency cheques there is usually a commission charge of one per cent of the amount changed. Both Thomas Cook and American Express sell euro travellers' cheques.

HEALTH, SAFETY & CRIME

As of 2006 the European Health Insurance Card (EHIC), valid for five years, replaces the E111 form. The Australian Medicare system also has a reciprocal health-care agreement.

Vaccinations are not required, and Italy does not present any serious health worries. Be aware, though, that it can become extremely hot in summer and it is sensible to protect yourself against the effects of this. Wear a hat and sunscreen whenever necessary, and ensure you keep well hydrated. Drink bottled water as opposed to tap water, and definitely avoid drinking from the city fountains. Most minor ailments can be diagnosed and treated at pharmacies (*farmacia*), identified throughout the city by the green cross sign. However, if you take prescriptive drugs, make sure you bring an adequate supply, as well as a letter from your doctor or personal health record card.

To all intents and purposes, Bologna is a safe city where the usual level of urban common sense will be sufficient to get you around without incident. Unlike other Italian cities to the south, there are no serious problems with street theft, muggings or drugs. That being said, the city is full of dark alleys and shadowy arcades, so take care when walking alone at night. If leaving a restaurant or club late at night it is usually best to take a taxi.

OPENING HOURS

Shop hours are usually 09.30–13.00 & 15.30 to 20.00. Many shops, restaurants, museums and galleries are closed for at least two weeks in August, some for the entire month.

Banks are open 08.30–13.30 and 14.30–15.30 on weekdays, closed Sat & Sun.

Attractions: opening hours for individual attractions are given next to their listing in the book.

PUBLIC TOILETS

If you must use public toilets, train and bus stations are the best options, although don't expect them to be spotless. Museums and galleries also have toilet facilities. Most cafés and restaurants have public facilities for patrons only, so you may have to buy a drink in order to use them. In some cases an attendant doles out *carta* (toilet paper) and expects a small tip in return. In Italy in general toilets run the gamut from clean and modern to a hole in the floor, so it's advisable to carry packets of sanitary wipes with you at all times.

CHILDREN

The Bolognese, like most Italians, love children, and are happy to cater to them in all manner of ways. As far as food goes, you will not go wrong with all the pasta choices, as well as pizza and, of course, ice cream. Restaurant chefs are usually very willing to prepare half portions of any dish.

To a child, all the churches, museums and libraries of Bologna and the surrounding towns can be boring, but the excellent book *Bologna for Kids*, with pages and pages of things to do and look for as they visit each church or museum, will keep them entertained. It's available from the tourist office (see page 150).

COMMUNICATIONS

The city's main post office is on the northern side of Piazza Minghetti, and is open 08.15–18.30 Mon–Fri, 08.15–13.00 Sat. The hours of business for smaller offices are 08.30–13.30 Mon–Sat. Italy's postal reputation is not high, so expect mail to take a little longer to reach the destination than it would from other European countries.

The city's dialling code is 051 and must be dialled before all numbers, even within the city. The code for Parma is 0521, for Ravenna 0544 and for Ferrara 0532. The prefix for Italy is +39.

Calling from Bologna

UK and Northern Ireland international access code + 44 + area code
Republic of Ireland international access code + 353 + area code
US & Canada international access code + 1 + area code
Australia international access code + 61 + area code
New Zealand international access code + 64 + area code

Calling Bologna from abroad

To call Bologna from abroad dial the access code 00 from the UK, Ireland and New Zealand, 011 from the US and Canada, 0011 from Australia, followed by the code for Italy 39, then the local number including the 051 code.

Mobile phones

In Italy mobile phones work on the GSM European standard. Before you leave home make sure you have made the necessary roaming arrangements with your company and find out what you will be charged for making and receiving calls. UK, New Zealand and Australian mobile phones will work in Italy, but US and Canadian cell phones will not. However, worth investigating are universal mobiles from rental companies. These mobiles work anywhere in the world with a permanent UK number that travels with you. Contact Mobal Rental in the UK at ☎ 1 543 426 999 ☎ 1 543 426 126; or in the US at ☎ 888 888 9162 (free call) or 212 785 5800 ⓦ www.mobalrental.com

Internet

The main internet cafés in the city are in the public library at Piazza Nettuno 3 and Via de Chiara 5, near Piazza San Stefano. Under Italy's new anti-terrorism legislation, picture ID is now required before you can use the internet.

ELECTRICITY

Italy functions on a 220V main supply. Travellers from the UK will need adaptors as Italian sockets are for plugs with two round pins. If coming from the US, purchase an adaptor before leaving home, as they are much more expensive in Bologna.

TRAVELLERS WITH DISABILITIES

In general Italy is still behind in catering for the disabled, but Bologna is better than most Italian cities. Contact an agency before departure for more details, such as Accessible Italy ⓦ www.accessibleitaly.com or Vacanze Serene ☎ 800 271 027.

FURTHER INFORMATION

Bologna's main IAT tourist office is located under the Palazzo Podestà at Piazza Maggiore. It provides more free maps and leaflets than you could possibly need. Within the same building is the Emporio della Cultura, which sells books, souvenirs and tickets for various events. Also here is the CST (Hotel Reservation Centre). There are tourist kiosks too at the railway station and the Arrivals terminal at the airport.

Bologna IAT Tourist Office ⓐ Piazza Maggiore 1 ① Tourist Hotline 246 541 ⓦ www.bolognaturismo.info ① 09.00–19.00 Mon–Sun

CST ① 800 856 065 ⓦ www.cst.bo.it

Museum passes (Bologna)

Abbonamento (a yearly pass) is good value if you're planning quite a long stay. For €25 it allows unlimited access to Bologna's museums. Visitors staying for a shorter period might find the *biglietto cumulativo* (one- or three-day passes) better value, costing €6–8. For €14 you can purchase a *biglietto integrato*, which is valid for three days and allows access to the museums and also use of public transport.

For further information contact the Municipality ① 203 040, or the tourist hotline ① 246 541 ① 09.00–19.00 Mon–Sat

△ *Mosaic in Ravenna's Church of San Vitale*

Useful phrases

Although English is spoken in many tourist locations in Bologna, these words and phrases may come in handy. See also the phrases for specific situations in other parts of this book.

English	Italian	*Approx. pronunciation*
BASICS		
Yes	Sì	*See*
No	No	*Noh*
Please	Per favore	*Perr fahvawreh*
Thank you	Grazie	*Grahtsyeh*
Hello	Salve	*Sahlveh*
Goodbye	Arrivederci	*Arreevehderrchee*
Excuse me	Scusi	*Skoozee*
Sorry	Scusi	*Skoozee*
That's okay	Va bene	*Vah behneh*
To	A	*Ah*
From	Da	*Dah*
I don't speak Italian	Non parlo italiano	*Nawn parrlaw itahlyahnaw*
Do you speak English?	Parla inglese?	*Parrla eenglehzeh?*
Good morning	Buon giorno	*Booawn geeyawrnaw*
Good afternoon	Buon pomeriggio	*Booawn pawmehreehdjaw*
Good evening	Buonasera	*Booawnah sehrah*
Goodnight	Buonanotte	*Booawnah nawtteh*
My name is ...	Mi chiamo ...	*Mee kyahmaw ...*
DAYS & TIMES		
Monday	Lunedì	*Loonehdee*
Tuesday	Martedì	*Marrtehdee*
Wednesday	Mercoledì	*Merrcawlehdee*
Thursday	Giovedì	*Jawvehdee*
Friday	Venerdì	*Venerrdee*
Saturday	Sabato	*Sahbahtaw*
Sunday	Domenica	*Dawmehneeca*
Morning	Mattino	*Mahtteenaw*
Afternoon	Pomeriggio	*Pawmehreedjaw*
Evening	Sera	*Sehra*
Night	Notte	*Notteh*
Yesterday	Ieri	*Yeree*

English	Italian	Approx. pronunciation
Today	Oggi	Odjee
Tomorrow	Domani	Dawmahnee
What time is it?	Che ore sono?	Keh awreh sawnaw?
It is …	Sono le …	Sawnaw leh …
09.00	Nove	Noveh
Midday	Mezzogiorno	Metsawjorrnaw
Midnight	Mezzanotte	Metsanotteh

NUMBERS

One	Uno	Oonaw
Two	Due	Dweh
Three	Tre	Treh
Four	Quattro	Kwahttraw
Five	Cinque	Cheenkweh
Six	Sei	Say
Seven	Sette	Setteh
Eight	Otto	Ottaw
Nine	Nove	Noveh
Ten	Dieci	Dyehchee
Eleven	Undici	Oondeechee
Twelve	Dodici	Dawdeechee
Twenty	Venti	Ventee
Fifty	Cinquanta	Cheenkwahnta
One hundred	Cento	Chentaw

MONEY

I would like to change these traveller's cheques/this currency	Vorrei cambiare questi assegni turistici/ questa valuta	Vawrray cahmbyahreh kwestee assenee tooree-steechee/kwesta vahloota
Where is the nearest ATM?	Dov'è il bancomat più vicino?	Dawveh eel bankomaht pyoo veecheenaw?
Do you accept credit cards?	Accettate carte di credito?	Achetahteh kahrrteh dee krehdeeitaw?

SIGNS & NOTICES

Airport	Aeroporto	Ahaerrhawpawrrtaw
Railway station	Stazione ferroviaria	Stahtsyawneh ferrawvyarya
Platform	Binario	Binahriaw
Smoking/ non-smoking	Per fumatori/ non fumatori	Perr foomahtawree/ non foomahtawree
Toilets	Gabinetti	Gabinettee
Ladies/Gentlemen	Signore/Signori	Seenyawreh/Seenyawree
Subway	Metropolitana	Metrawpawleetahna

Emergencies

Police ❶ 113 **Fire ❶** 115, **Ambulance ❶** 333 333 or 118
Lost property ❶ 601 8626

MEDICAL SERVICES
Accident and emergency

By law, all hospital accident and emergency rooms must treat all emergency cases for free. If you need urgent medical care go to the *pronto soccorso* (casualty department). All the hospitals listed below offer 24-hour casualty services.

Hospitals

Ospedale Bellaria ❸ Via Altura 3 **❶** 622 5111 **◎** Bus 36, 90
Ospedale Maggiore ❷ Largo Nigrisoli 2 **❶** 647 8111 **◎** Bus 13, 81, 86, 87, 91, 92, 93
Ospedale Santa Orsola-Malpighi, the city's main hospital.
❸ Via Massarenti 9, east of the city **❶** 6363 111 **◎** Bus 25, 34, 36, 94

Dentists

Contact the main hospital (see above) or look in the Pagine Gialle (Yellow Pages) under *Dentisti*.

Doctors

EU nationals with a European Health Insurance Card (EHIC) can consult a national health service doctor free of charge, with any drugs prescribed bought at chemists at prices set by the Health Ministry. Tests and outpatient treatment are charged at fixed rates

▶ *Children chase the pigeons in Palazzo Comunale*

also. Non-EU nationals who consult a health service doctor will be charged a fee at the doctor's discretion, so make sure you have adequate health insurance.

Opticians
Replacement lenses can usually be fitted overnight, and most opticians will replace a missing screw or make adjustments on the spot. See also *Ottica* in the Pagine Gialle (Yellow Pages).

Pharmacies
Farmacias (pharmacies) are identified by a green cross. Italian pharmacists are well qualified to give informal medical advice as well as dispensing prescriptions. Make sure you know the generic as well as the brand name of your regular medicines, as they may be sold under a different name in Italy.

EMERGENCY PHRASES

Help! Aiuto! *Ahyootaw!*   **Fire!** Al fuoco! *Ahl fooawcaw!*   **Stop!** Ferma! *Fairmah!*

Call an ambulance/a doctor/the police/the fire service! Chiamate un'ambulanza/un medico/la polizia/i pompieri! *Kyahmahteh oon ahmboolahntsa/oon mehdeecaw/la pawleetsya/ee pompee-ehree!*

Pharmacies (late-night)

There is a large 24-hour pharmacy in the Piazza Maggiore, the Farmacia Comunale. If it's closed, a list on the door has details of the rotation of open pharmacies. ⓐ Piazza Maggiore 6 ⓘ 239 690 Ⓝ Bus 11, 20, 29, 30

For an emergency pharmacist or for late-night delivery of medication, call the Farmaco Pronto ⓣ 800 218 489

The publishers would like to thank the following individuals and organisations for supplying the copyright photographs for this book. Barbara Rogers: all photographs except: Arcoveggio Hotel (page 38); Bologna Turismo (pages 19, 23, 65/Alessandro Salomoni, 84, 91/Alessandro Salomoni, 98); Centro Turistico Città di Bologna (page 41); Fototeca ENIT (pages 5, 108/Vito Arcomano, page 112/Paulo Ghirotti); Pictures Colour Library (pages 42–3); Robert Harding (pages 31, 102); Timothy Sewter (page 70); Tourist Information Office, Ferrara (pages 15, 105); Teatro Comunale Bologna (page 90); World Pictures (pages 51, 69).

Copy editor: Penny Isaac
Proofreader: Jan McCann

Send your thoughts to
books@thomascook.com

- Found a great bar, club, shop or must-see sight that we don't feature?

- Like to tip us off about any information that needs updating?

- Want to tell us what you love about this handy little guidebook and more importantly how we can make it even handier?

Then here's your chance to tell all! Send us ideas, discoveries and recommendations today and then look out for your valuable input in the next edition of this title. As an extra 'thank you' from Thomas Cook Publishing, you'll be automatically entered into our exciting monthly prize draw.

Send an email to the above address (stating the book's title) or write to: CitySpots Project Editor, Thomas Cook Publishing, PO Box 227, The Thomas Cook Business Park, Unit 18, Coningsby Road, Peterborough PE3 8SB, UK.